HAMILTON COLLEGE
D0234253
HAMILTON COLLEGE

Spotting Shells

An introduction to seashells of the world

Graham D. Saunders
Honorary Secretary of The British Shell Collectors' Club

Photography by Mike Freeman

Illustrated by Andy Martin

USBORNE

Contents

3 What is a shell?
4 How to use this book
6 Gastropods
37 Bivalves
47 Chitons and Tusk Shells
48 Cephalopods
49 Parts of a shell
50 How shells grow
51 Biology of a mollusc
52 Life cycle of a mollusc
53 How a mollusc moves
54 Rocky and sandy shores
56 Muddy shores and coral
57 Collecting and storing shells
59 Books to read
Useful addresses
60 Glossary
61 Scorecard
63 Index

Designed by
Cloud Nine Design

Edited by
Helen Gilks and
Lauris Morgan-Griffiths

First published in 1979 by
Usborne Publishing Limited,
20 Garrick Street, London WC2

Text and Artwork © 1979 by
Usborne Publishing Limited

All rights reserved. No part of this publication may be reproduced, stored in a retrieval system, or transmitted by any means, electronic, mechanical, photocopying, recording, or otherwise, without the prior permission of the publisher.

Made and printed in Great Britain by
Purnell & Sons Ltd, Paulton (Bristol) and London

HAMILTON
COLLEGE

What is a shell?

HAMILTON

Shells are the protective covering of soft-bodied animals called molluscs. The name mollusc comes from the Latin *mollis* meaning soft. When the animals that live inside shells die, the shells are left free to drift in the sea. Many of them are washed up on the seashore. This book helps you to identify some of the many thousands of different kinds of sea shells that are found all over the world.

Classes

Over the millions of years molluscs have evolved in different ways. Scientists have divided them into six "Classes". Each Class has a distinct type of shell. The five major Classes are:

1. Gastropoda
(Snails, limpets, whelks, etc.)
Gastropods have a single shell which is usually coiled.

2. Bivalvia

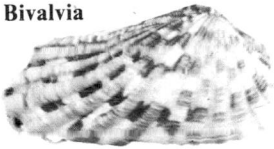

(Cockles, mussels, oysters, etc.)
Bivalves have two shells (valves) usually unequal in size, and joined by a hinge.

3. Cephalopoda
(Squid, octopus, cuttle-fish).
Some cephalopods have no shell; in others the shell is outside the animal, or inside the animal's soft body. They all have tentacles.

4. Amphineura
(Chitons) have a flexible shell made up of eight overlapping plates.

5. Scaphopoda

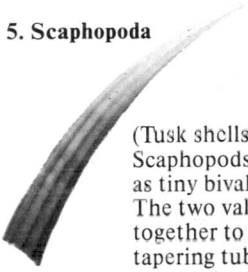

(Tusk shells).
Scaphopods begin life as tiny bivalves.
The two valves fuse together to form a tapering tube which is open at both ends.

This book shows examples of the first five of the six Classes. When you find a shell, first decide which of these Classes it belongs to and turn to that section in the book. Flick through until you see a shell similar to the one you have found.

In each section of the book you will find several individual species, or kinds, of shells. We cannot show all the different species of shells that exist in the world (there are about 100,000), so we have shown only a selection.

How to use this book

What is a species?
All the species in this book are molluscs, but they are organized, or classified, into smaller groups to show their similarities.

Molluscs are divided first into Classes, then families, genera (singular "genus") and finally into species. Classification does not only depend on the similarity in appearance of the shells, but on the biology and behaviour of the animal.

Each individual shell is a separate **species.** Shells of the same species breed together and nearly always look the same. A group of species which look similar but do not breed together is called a **genus.** A group of genera that have similar characteristics but do not necessarily look alike is called a **family.**

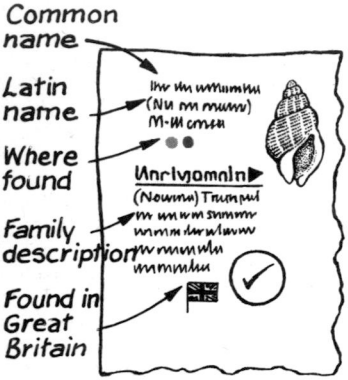

Why use Latin names?
Latin names are used because in many cases there is no common name for a shell. Common names change; the Latin name never does.

The Latin name of a family almost always ends in "idae." The Latin name of a species is made up of two words. The first word is the genus name, and starts with a capital letter. The second is the name of the particular species and starts with a small letter.

What's on a page.
On each page is a description of a family. When you find a shell that looks like the one you want to identify, read the description to check that your shell belongs to that family. The description tells you the common name and the Latin name, where those shells are found, and a general description of their colour and shape.

See page 49 for a labelled drawing showing the different features of a shell.

Beside each family description there is a blank circle. If your shell belongs to that family, tick it off.

At the back of the book is a scorecard which gives a score for every family you find.

Below each family description is a symbol of a flag. This shows which shell families can be found in Britain. Some families cannot be found here, but you may see them in a shell shop or museum.

In addition to the family description, there is a small caption next to each species illustrated. This gives its common and Latin name, maximum size and a coloured circle to show where in the world it can be found (see page 5).

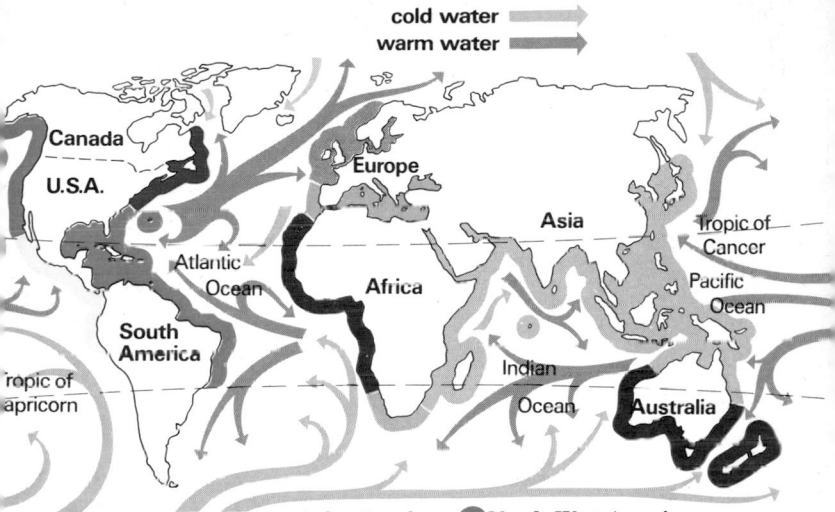

The description for each family of shells tells you what type of water that family prefers: tropical, warm or cold. Tropical means in the area between the two tropics (see above). The warm and cold regions of the seas are marked on the map.

Different species that are members of the same family of shells will generally be found living in similar conditions - cold or warm water - although one species may live in one part of the world, and another thousands of miles away.

You can find out where the species illustrated in this book live by looking at the small coloured circles after the name of the species. These colours refer to the areas of the world shown on the map.

Indo-Pacific. Warm to tropical waters. A large number of colourful and attractive species. Probably the richest area in the world for shells.

Australia and New Zealand. Many different families and species; many of them colourful.

North-West America. Cool waters. Shells tend to be hardy and strong. A few are colourful.

Panamic. Warm waters. Rich in colourful shells. Fewer species than in Indo-Pacific.

Caribbean. Warm waters. Many different species. Some of the largest species of shells are from this area.

North-East America. Temperate to cold waters. Shells tend to be strong and heavy. Large numbers are white or brown.

North-West Europe. Cool waters, in places warm because of Gulf Stream. Few colourful shells.

Mediterranean. Warm waters. A few colourful shells, generally rather small.

West Africa. Sub-tropical to tropical waters. Shells of this area are fast-growing and many are colourful.

South Africa. Cool waters. Strong shells, several colourful species.

Keyhole Limpets

(Fissurellidae). Tropical and warm seas.
Cap-shaped shells; most species have a small keyhole shape in the top.
On rocks, near low water line.

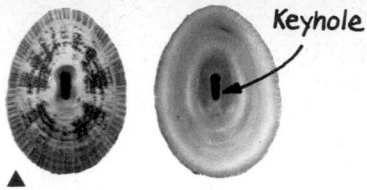

▲ **Green Panama Keyhole**
(Fissurella virescens)
4cm.

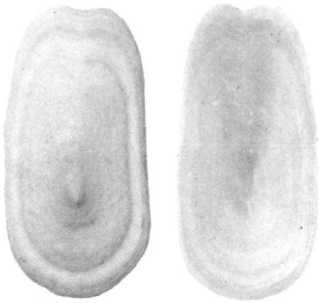

Roman Shield ▶
(Scutus antipodes)
10cm. Australia

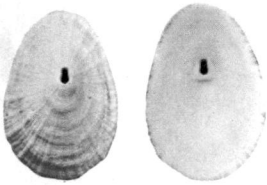

◀ **Italian Keyhole**
(Diodora italica)
5cm.

Limpets

(Patellidae). Warm and tropical seas. Flattened cone-shaped shells, evenly shaped. More pointed shells come from rough waters. Several hundred species.

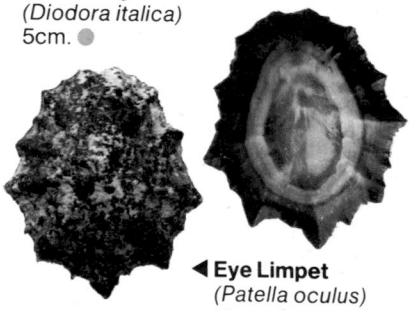

◀ **Eye Limpet**
(Patella oculus)
10cm.

▲ **Mediterranean Limpet**
(Patella caerulea)
6cm.

Tortoiseshell Limpet ▼
(Acmea testudinalis)
2.5cm

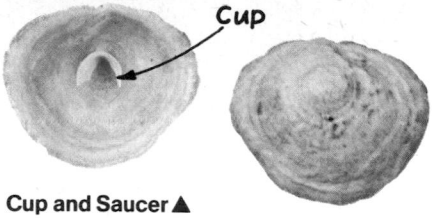

Cup and Saucer ▲
(Cheila equestris)
2.5cm.

Hoof Shells

(Hipponicidae) Worldwide. Cap-shaped, non-spiral shells. Found in shallow waters. White shells usually stained yellow or brown. Often attached to other shells.

◀ **Horse's Hoof**
(Amalthea antiquata)
2cm

Slipper Limpets/Crucibles

(Calyptraeidae) Worldwide. Flattened shells, often non-spiral. Thin shelf inside the shell. Often attached to other shells or stones. Smooth and evenly shaped.

▲
Hungarian Cap
(Capulus ungaricus)
5cm.

Slipper Limpet ▼
(Crepidula fornicata)
5cm.

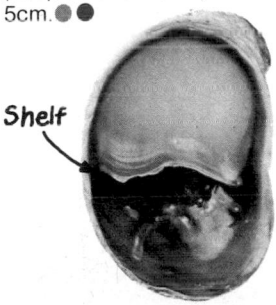

▲
Peruvian Hat
(Trochatella trochiformis)
7cm

Carrier Shells

(Xenophoridae). Warm and tropical seas. Have a thin horny operculum. Cement dead shells and rubble to the surface of the shell.

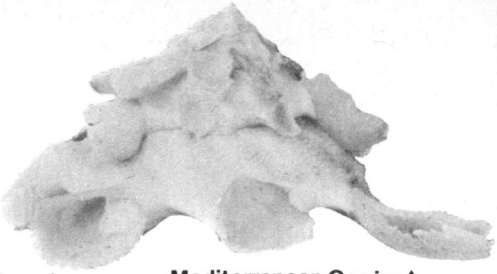

Mediterranean Carrier▲
(Xenophora crispa)
5cm.

Dead shells

▲ Pallid Carrier
(Xenophora pallidula)
10cm.

◀ Violet Snails

(Janthinidae). Warm and tropical seas. Thin and fragile globe-like shells. Normally violet or white in colour.
Small notch on outer lip.

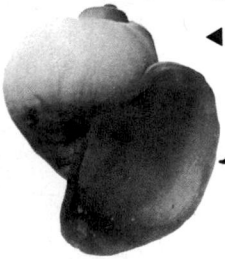

◀ Dwarf Purple Snail
(Janthina exigua)
2cm.

Notch on outer lip

Giant Sundial▶
(Architectonica maxima)
8cm.

Sundials▶

(Architectonicidae). Warm and tropical seas. Thin shell with large flattened spiral. The inside of the spiral is lined with small knobbly ridges.

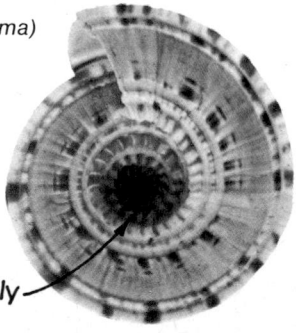

Knobbly ridge

Ormers/Ear Shells

(Haliotidae). All warm and tropical seas except Caribbean. Flat shells with a spiral whorl and a row of tiny breathing holes. Mother-of-pearl on inside of shell.

▲ **Black Ormer**
(Haliotis cracherodi)
21cm.

Breathing holes

Ridged Ear Shell
(Haliotis scalaris)
10cm. W. Australia

Mother-of-pearl

Turban and Star Shells

(Turbinidae). Tropical and warm seas. Medium to large shells. Found lower on the beach than Top Shells. Heavy spiral operculum. About 500 species.

Tapestry Turban ▶
(Turbo petholatus)
8cm. Australia

Heavy operculum

◀ **Modest Star Shell**
(Astraea modesta)
5cm. Japan

Top Shells (p. 10-11)

(Trochidae). Worldwide. Shells from deep water are pointed and thin with fine surface sculpture; shells from shallow water are heavy and rounded. Round, horny operculum. Inside the shell is mother-of-pearl.

Pyramid Top Shell▲
(Tectus pyramis)
10cm.

▲
Yellow Sponge Top Shell
(Calliostoma monile)
2.5cm. N. Australia

Radiant Top Shell▼
(Trochus radiatus)
4cm. Indian Ocean

◀ Kelp Top Shell
(Calliostoma bonita)
3cm.

Snake Skin Top Shell▶
(Tegula pellisserpentis)
3cm.

◀ **Coral Top**
(Gibbula corallinoides)
2.5cm. ●

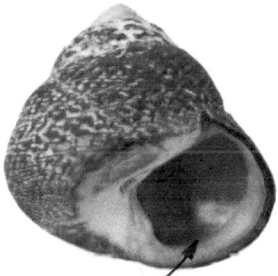

Lined Top▶
(Monodonta lineata)
3cm. ●

Mother-of-pearl

Strawberry Top▶
(Clanculus pharonium)
2.5cm. Indian Ocean ●

▲
Pheasant Shell
(Phasianella ventricosa)
3cm. ●

Dolphin Shell▶
(Angaria delphinula)
8cm. ●

Periwinkles/Winkles

(Littorinidae). Worldwide. Cold-water shells are rounded and heavy. Tropical shells are thinner and high-spired.

▲ **Southern Periwinkle**
(Littorina angulifera)
3cm.

Flat Periwinkle ▶
(Littorina littoralis)
1.5cm.

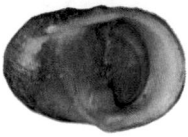

▲ **Chameleon Nerite**
(Nerita chameleon)
3cm. Australia

Nerite Snails

(Neritidae). Tropical and warm seas. Strong and often colourful. Broad body whorl. Hook on operculum.

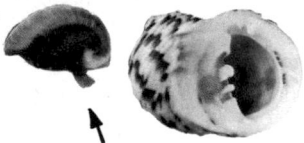

◀ **Bleeding Tooth**
(Nerita peloronta)
4cm.

Hook on operculum

Turrets/Screw Shells ▶

(Turritellidae). Warm and tropical seas. Long thin spiral shells live buried in sand or mud below low water line.

◀ **European Screw Shell**
(Turitella communis)
4cm.

Round opening

◀ **Common Cerith**
(Cerithum vulgatum)
8cm.

◀ **Horn Shells/Needle Whelks**

(Cerithidae). Worldwide, but more common in tropical seas. Identified by siphonal canal which twists back.
Moves about on weed or rock.

Banded Creeper ▶
(Rhinoclavis fasciatus)
8cm.

Precious Wentletrap ▶
(Epitonium scalare)
7.5cm.

Wentletraps ▶

(Epitoniidae). Worldwide. Round opening. Colour white, grey or brown with thin, round, dark-coloured operculum.
Notice ribs on shell.

◀ **Crenulated Wentletrap**
(Opalia crenata)
3cm.

Lance Auger ▶
(Terebra lanceata)
8cm. W. Pacific

◀ **Augers**

(Terebridae). Tropical and warm seas. Long, thin spire. Augers distinguished from Turret and Horn shells by shape of siphonal canal.

Knorr's Worm ▲
(Vermicularia knorri)
10cm. ●

◀ Worm Shells

(Vermetidae). Warm and tropical seas. Young shells shaped like pointed turrets, but then grow unevenly into "worm-like" shapes. About 50 species.

Turrids ▶

(Turridae). Worldwide. Small shells with notch at the suture. Small opening. Horny operculum. More than 1,200 species. Up to 15 cm.

◀ Rose Turrid
(Clavus rosalina)
4cm. ●

Notch

Tun Shells

(Tonnidae). Tropical and warm seas. Large thin shells with spiral ridges. Colour white, yellow or brown. Often damaged when found on beaches.

◀ Partridge Tun
(Tonna perdix)
20cm. ●

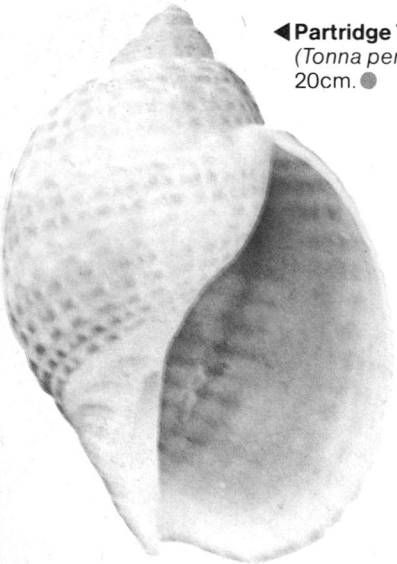

Banded Tun ▼
(Tonna sulcosa)
12cm. ●

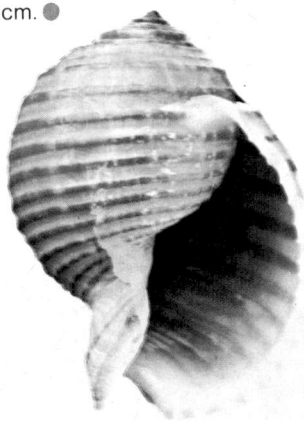

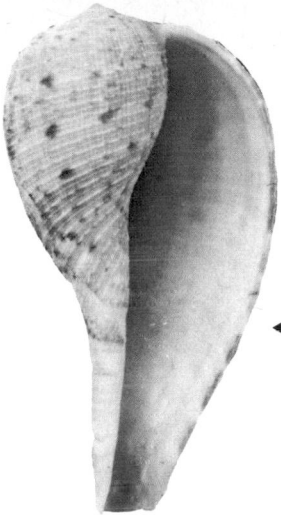

◀ **Fig Shells**

(Ficidae). Tropical seas, except W. Africa. Long siphonal canal. Finely sculptured with criss-crossed surface. Less than 15 species.

◀ **Spotted Fig**
(Ficus ficoides)
10cm. ●

Moon Snails/Necklace Shells

(Naticidae). Worldwide. Strong, shiny shells which can be thick, rounded or flattened. Small spire with few whorls. Large opening. Operculum is usually semicircular.

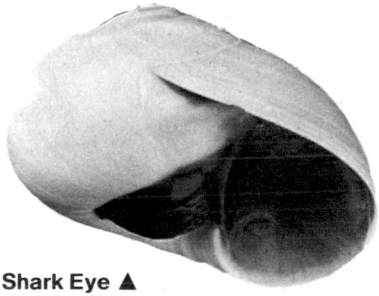

Shark Eye ▲
(Polinices duplicatus)
8cm ● ●

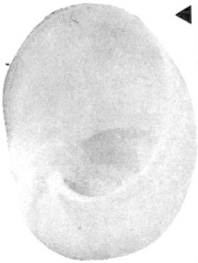

◀ **Baby Ear**
(Sinum perspectivum)
4cm. ● ●

Colourful Atlantic Moon Snail ▶
(Naticarius canrena)
4cm. ● ●

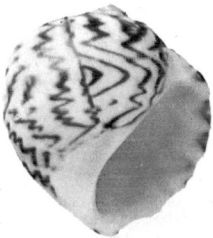

◀ **Lightning Moon Shell**
(Natica fulminea)
3cm. ●

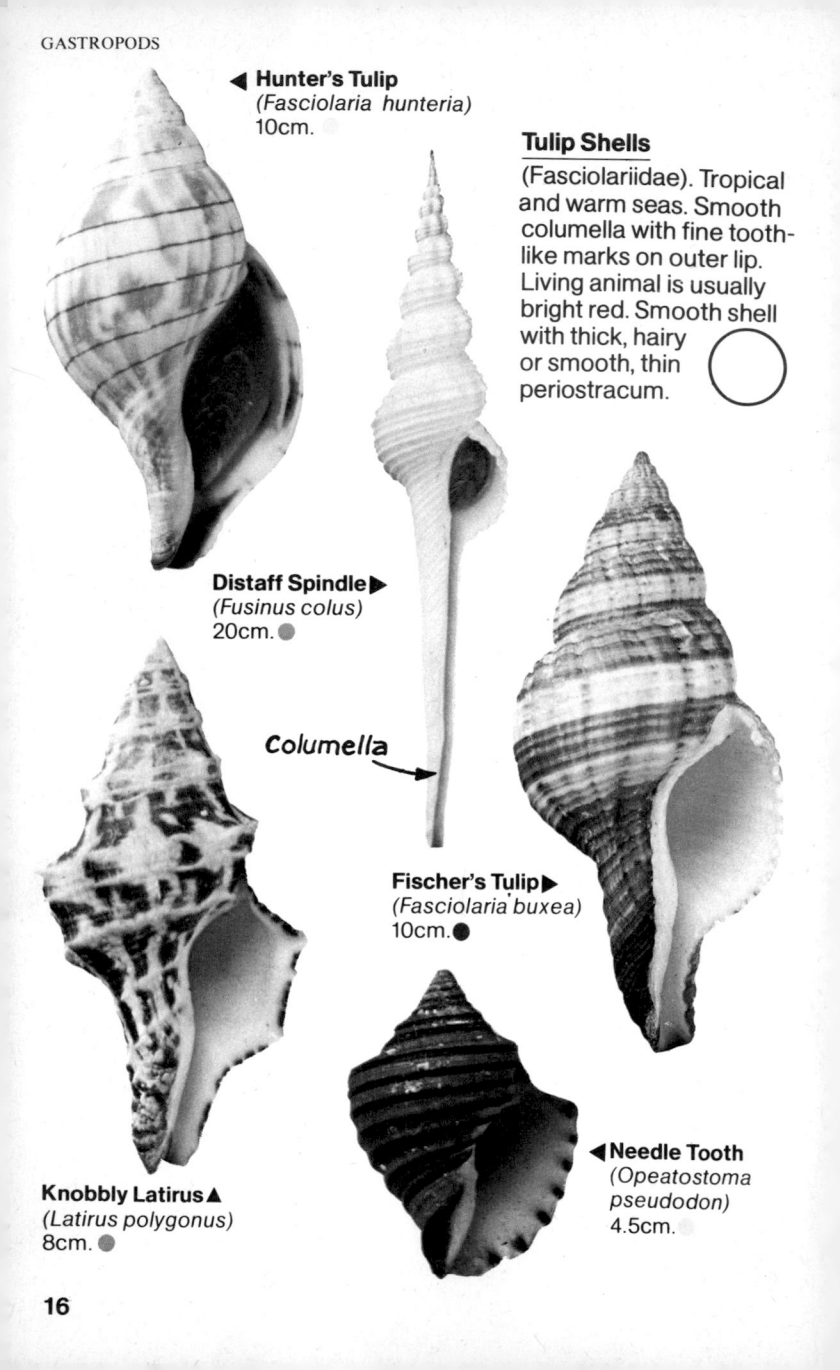

◀ **Hunter's Tulip**
(Fasciolaria hunteria)
10cm.

Tulip Shells

(Fasciolariidae). Tropical and warm seas. Smooth columella with fine tooth-like marks on outer lip. Living animal is usually bright red. Smooth shell with thick, hairy or smooth, thin periostracum.

Distaff Spindle▶
(Fusinus colus)
20cm.

Fischer's Tulip▶
(Fasciolaria buxea)
10cm.

Knobbly Latirus▲
(Latirus polygonus)
8cm.

◀ **Needle Tooth**
(Opeatostoma pseudodon)
4.5cm.

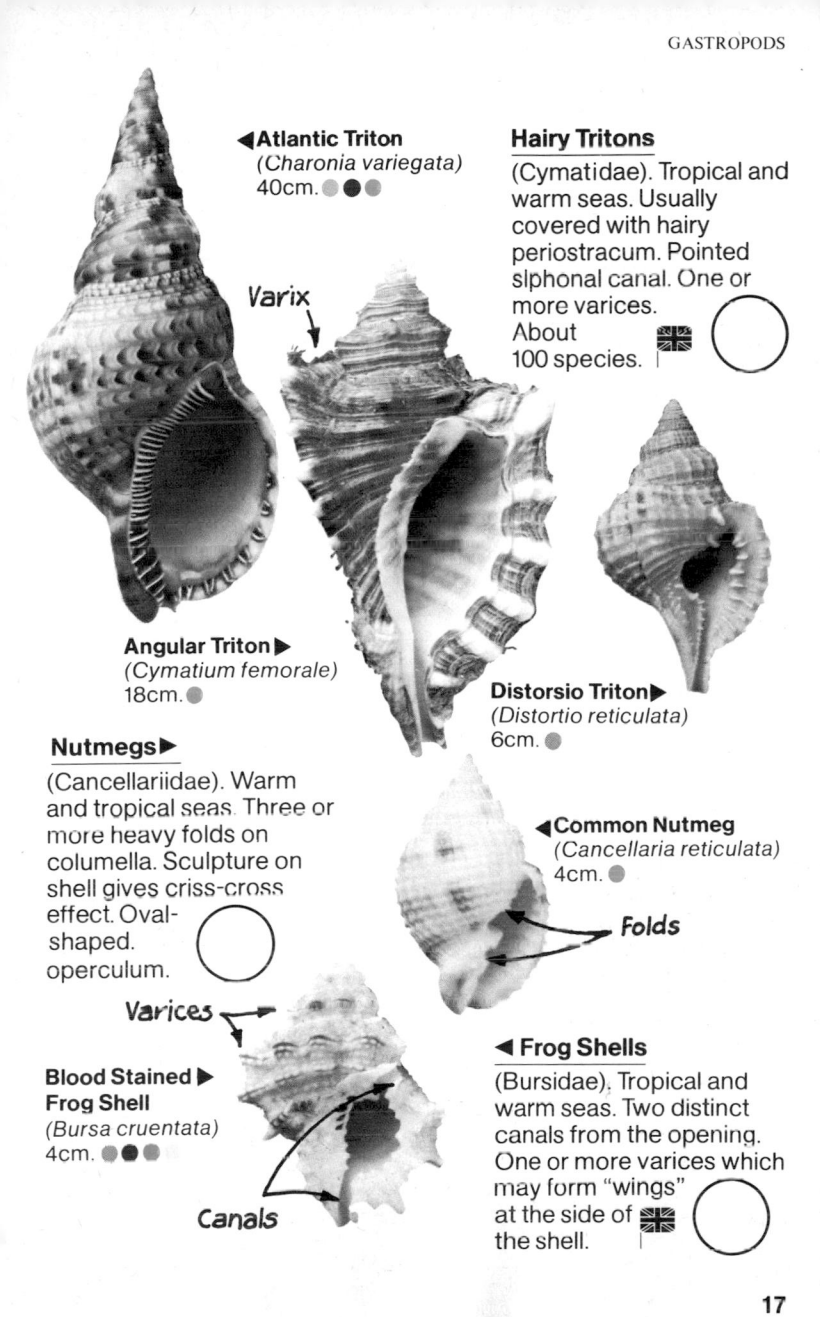

◀**Atlantic Triton**
(Charonia variegata)
40cm.

Hairy Tritons

(Cymatidae). Tropical and warm seas. Usually covered with hairy periostracum. Pointed siphonal canal. One or more varices. About 100 species.

Angular Triton▶
(Cymatium femorale)
18cm.

Distorsio Triton▶
(Distortio reticulata)
6cm.

Nutmegs▶

(Cancellariidae). Warm and tropical seas. Three or more heavy folds on columella. Sculpture on shell gives criss-cross effect. Oval-shaped. operculum.

◀**Common Nutmeg**
(Cancellaria reticulata)
4cm.

Blood Stained▶
Frog Shell
(Bursa cruentata)
4cm.

◀ **Frog Shells**

(Bursidae). Tropical and warm seas. Two distinct canals from the opening. One or more varices which may form "wings" at the side of the shell.

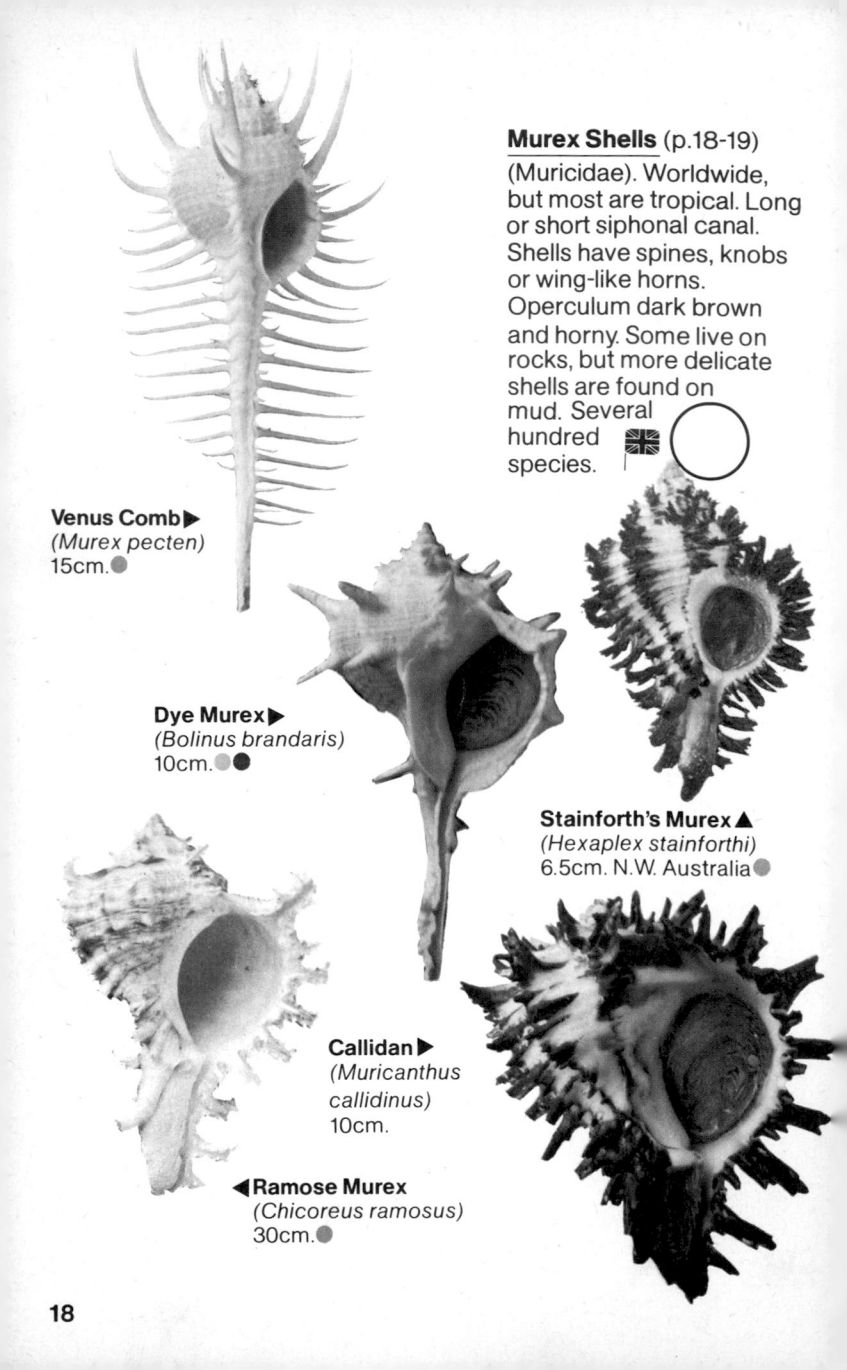

Murex Shells (p.18-19)

(Muricidae). Worldwide, but most are tropical. Long or short siphonal canal. Shells have spines, knobs or wing-like horns. Operculum dark brown and horny. Some live on rocks, but more delicate shells are found on mud. Several hundred species.

Venus Comb▶
(Murex pecten)
15cm.

Dye Murex▶
(Bolinus brandaris)
10cm.

Stainforth's Murex▲
(Hexaplex stainforthi)
6.5cm. N.W. Australia

Callidan▶
(Muricanthus callidinus)
10cm.

◀**Ramose Murex**
(Chicoreus ramosus)
30cm.

◀ **Leafy Horn Mouth**
(Ceratostoma foliatus)
10cm.

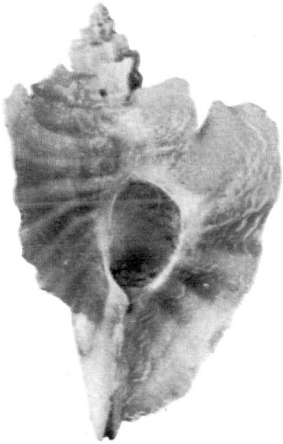

Three Winged Rock Shell ▶
(Pteropurpura trialata)
8.5cm

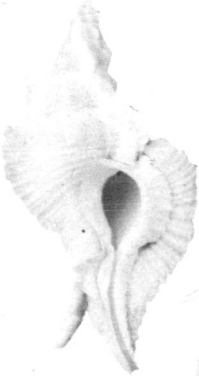

◀ **Murex Pinnatus**
(Pterynotus alatus)
7cm. S.E. Asia

▲
Cuming's Typhis
(Typhis cumingi)
2.5cm.

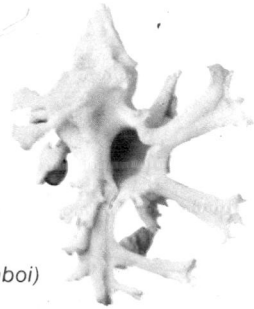

Zambo's Murex ▶
(Homalocantha zamboi)
6cm. Philippines

Rock Shells/Dye Shells

(Thaididae). Worldwide. Solid, low-spired shells with a large body whorl. Wide opening. Operculum red/brown, thin and horny. Usually small knobs around the shell. On rocks between high and low water.

◀ **Garland Thaid**
(Nassa serta)
7cm. E. Australia ●

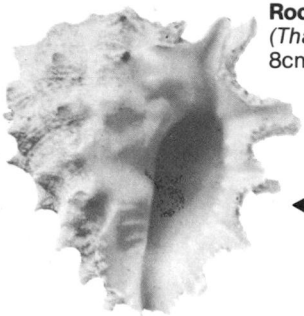

Rock Shell ▶
(Thais haemastoma)
8cm. ●●●

◀ **Red Mouth Drupe**
(Drupa rubusidaea)
5.5cm. ●

Wide Mouth Rock Shell ▶
(Purpura patula)
10cm. ●

◀ **Cart Rut Shell**
(Neothais scalaris)
10cm. New Zealand ●

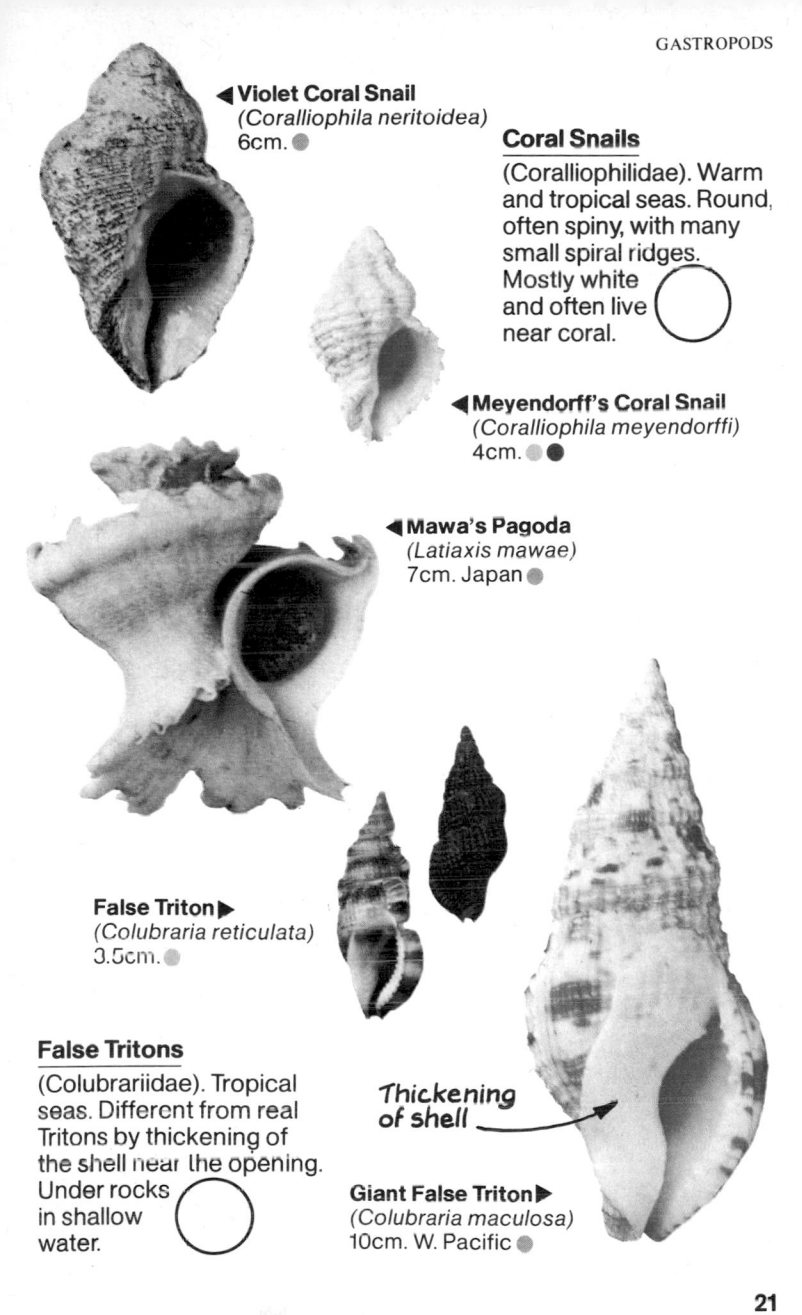

◀ **Violet Coral Snail**
(Coralliophila neritoidea)
6cm.

Coral Snails

(Coralliophilidae). Warm and tropical seas. Round, often spiny, with many small spiral ridges. Mostly white and often live near coral.

◀ **Meyendorff's Coral Snail**
(Coralliophila meyendorffi)
4cm.

◀ **Mawa's Pagoda**
(Latiaxis mawae)
7cm. Japan

False Triton ▶
(Colubraria reticulata)
3.5cm.

False Tritons

(Colubrariidae). Tropical seas. Different from real Tritons by thickening of the shell near the opening. Under rocks in shallow water.

Giant False Triton ▶
(Colubraria maculosa)
10cm. W. Pacific

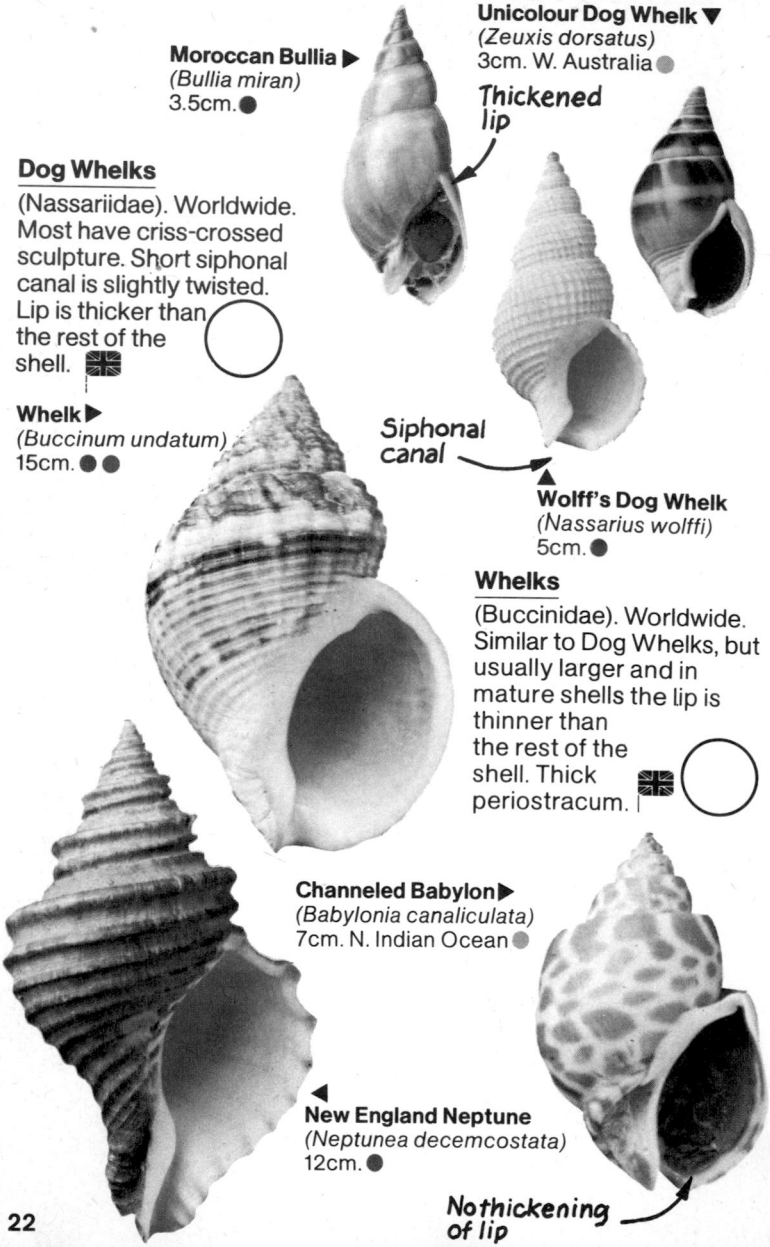

Moroccan Bullia ▶
(Bullia miran)
3.5cm. ●

Unicolour Dog Whelk ▼
(Zeuxis dorsatus)
3cm. W. Australia ●

Dog Whelks

(Nassariidae). Worldwide. Most have criss-crossed sculpture. Short siphonal canal is slightly twisted. Lip is thicker than the rest of the shell.

Whelk ▶
(Buccinum undatum)
15cm. ● ●

▲
Wolff's Dog Whelk
(Nassarius wolffi)
5cm. ●

Whelks

(Buccinidae). Worldwide. Similar to Dog Whelks, but usually larger and in mature shells the lip is thinner than the rest of the shell. Thick periostracum.

Channeled Babylon ▶
(Babylonia canaliculata)
7cm. N. Indian Ocean ●

◀
New England Neptune
(Neptunea decemcostata)
12cm. ●

Helmet Shells

(Cassidae). Tropical seas. Large, heavy shells often with wide strong lips. Teeth on one or both lips. Siphonal canal twists and turns backwards. About 80 species.

King Helmet ▲
(Cassis tuberosa)
23cm.

Canal twists backwards

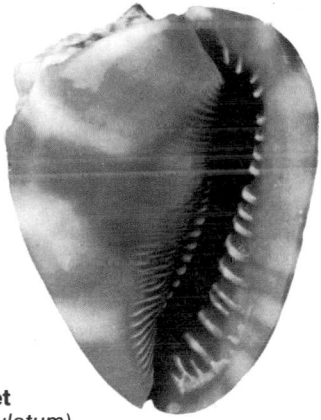

Bull Mouth ▶
(Cypraecassis rufa)
18cm.

◀ Scotch Bonnet
(Phalium granulatum)
7cm.

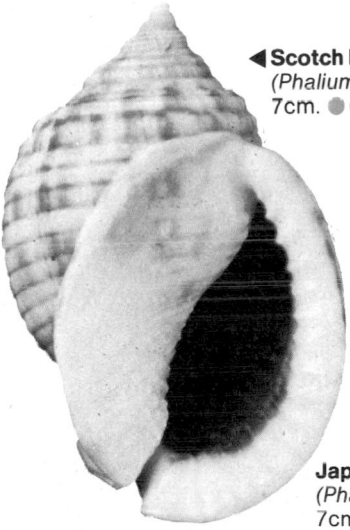

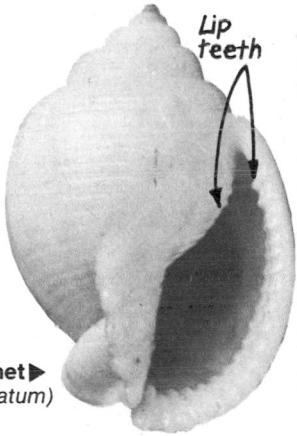

Japanese Bonnet ▶
(Phalium bisulcatum)
7cm.

Strombs/Conches (p. 24-25)

(Strombidae). Tropical and warm seas. Young shells can be mistaken for Cone Shells before they have developed their strong, broad, often wing-like outer lip. Have notch at the side, known as "stromboid notch". Living animal has brightly coloured eyes on long stalks.

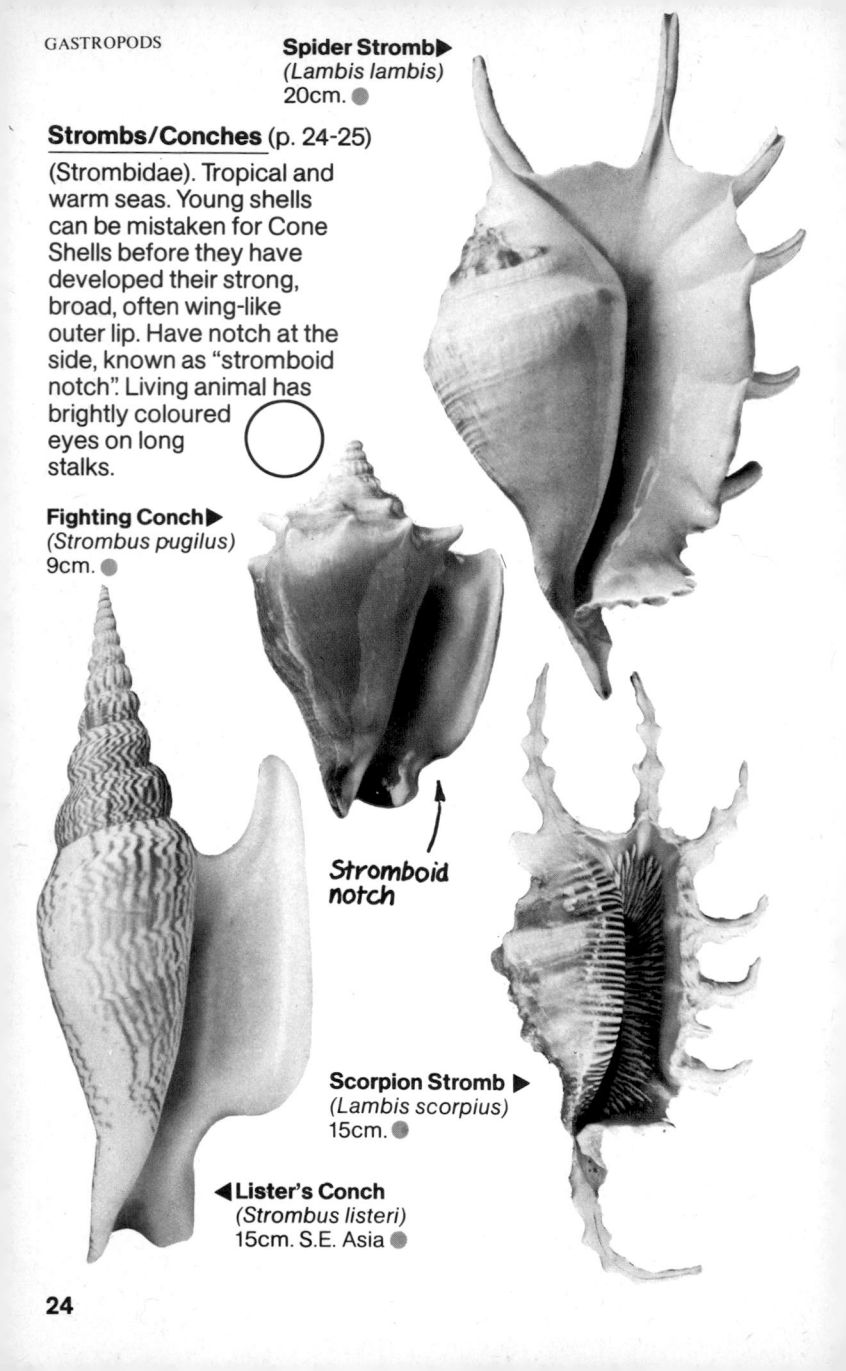

Spider Stromb▶
(Lambis lambis)
20cm.

Fighting Conch▶
(Strombus pugilus)
9cm.

Scorpion Stromb ▶
(Lambis scorpius)
15cm.

◀Lister's Conch
(Strombus listeri)
15cm. S.E. Asia

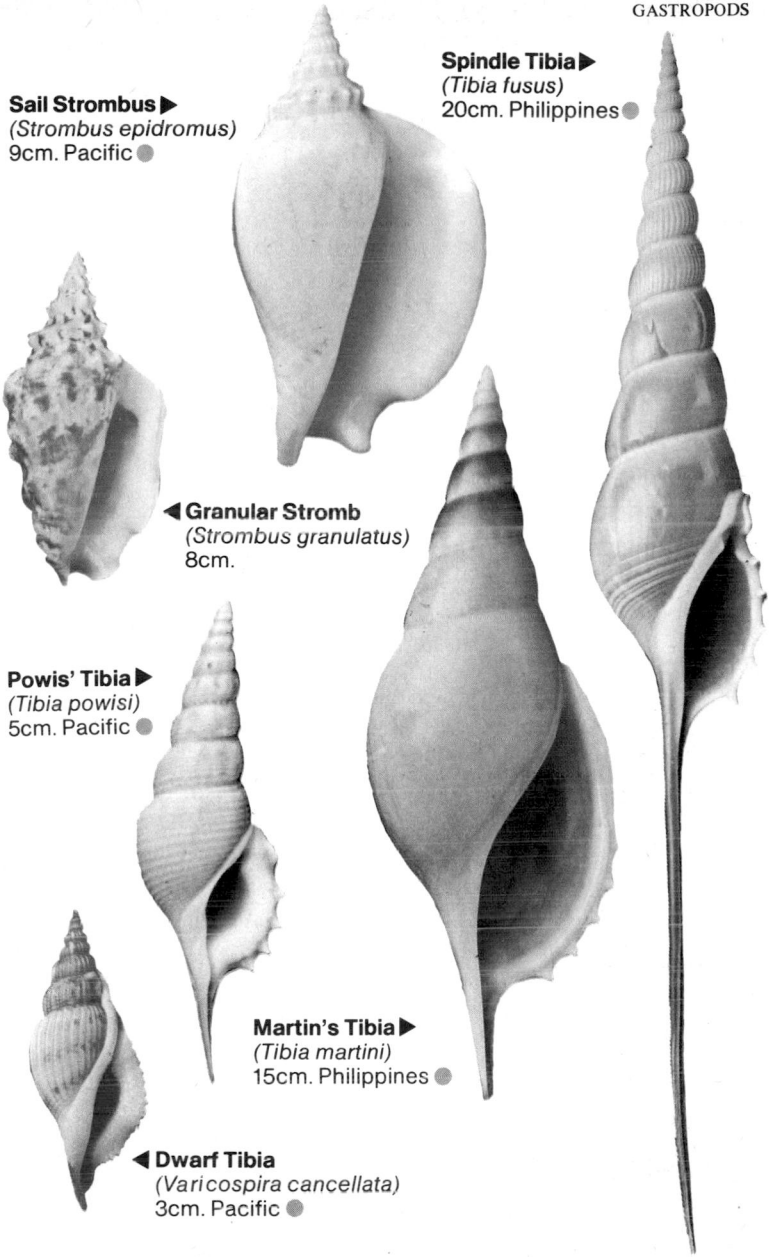
Sail Strombus ▶
(Strombus epidromus)
9cm. Pacific
Spindle Tibia ▶
(Tibia fusus)
20cm. Philippines
◀ Granular Stromb
(Strombus granulatus)
8cm.
Powis' Tibia ▶
(Tibia powisi)
5cm. Pacific
Martin's Tibia ▶
(Tibia martini)
15cm. Philippines
◀ Dwarf Tibia
(Varicospira cancellata)
3cm. Pacific

Ostrich Foot Shells ▶

(Struthiolaridae). New Zealand, Australia and Indian Ocean. Fragile, brown shells with thickened lip. Heavy white thickening by opening.

◀ Ostrich Foot
(Struthiolaria papulosa)
9cm. New Zealand●

West African Bird Foot ▶
(Aporrhais senegalensis)
3cm.●

Pelican Foot/Duck Foot Shells

(Aporrhaidae). N. Atlantic, Mediterranean, W. Africa. Wide lip, usually with straight spines. Only 5 to 6 living species.

◀ Pelican's Foot
(Aporrhais pespelicani)
6cm.●●

Snipe Head ▶
(Tudicula inermis)
8cm. N.W. Australia●

Vase Shells

(Vasidae). Tropical seas. Heavy shells, usually white with dark markings on their blunt spines. Has a hairy periostracum.

Vase Shell ▶
(Vasum muricatum)
13cm.●

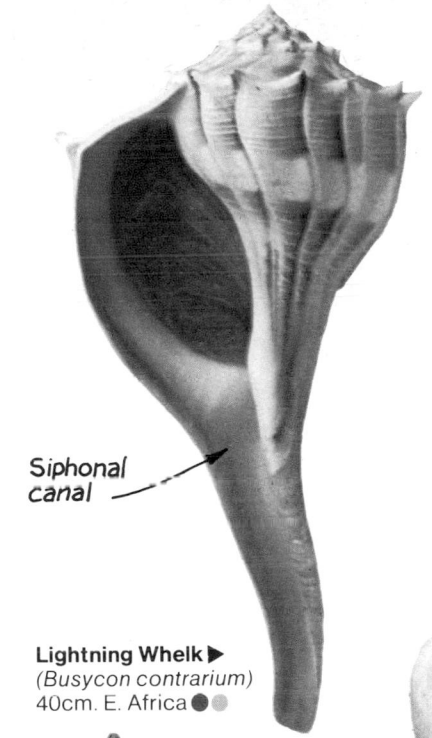

Crown Conches

(Melongenidae). Tropical seas. Short-spired heavy shell with long siphonal canal. Periostracum is usually thick and rather rubbery. Feeds on other molluscs.

Lightning Whelk ▶
(Busycon contrarium)
40cm. E. Africa ●●

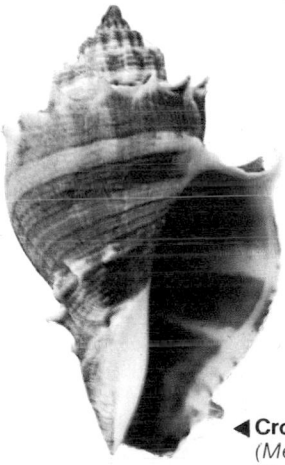

◀ Crown Conch
(Melongena corona)
10cm. ●

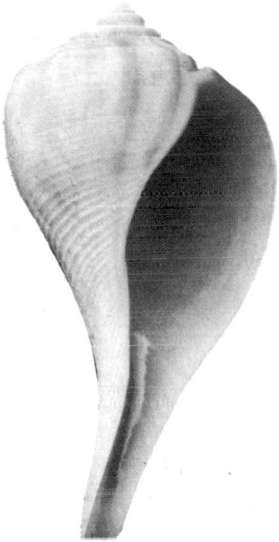

▲
Fig Whelk
(Busycon spiratum)
13cm. ●●

◀ **Rose Harp**
(Harpa doris)
7.5cm.●

Harp Shells

(Harpidae). Tropical seas. Attractive shells with obvious varices which show growth stages. About 12 species.

Articulated Harp ▶
(Harpa articularis)
10cm. W. Pacific●

Cone Shells

(Conidae). Tropical seas. Evenly-shaped cone or cylinder-type shells with long, narrow opening. Some have poisonous sting.

Court Cone ▶
(Conus aulicus)
7cm.●

◀ **Fig Cone**
(Conus figulinus)
8cm.●

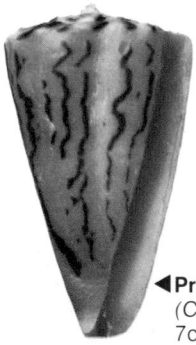

◀ **Prince Cone**
(Conus princeps)
7cm.

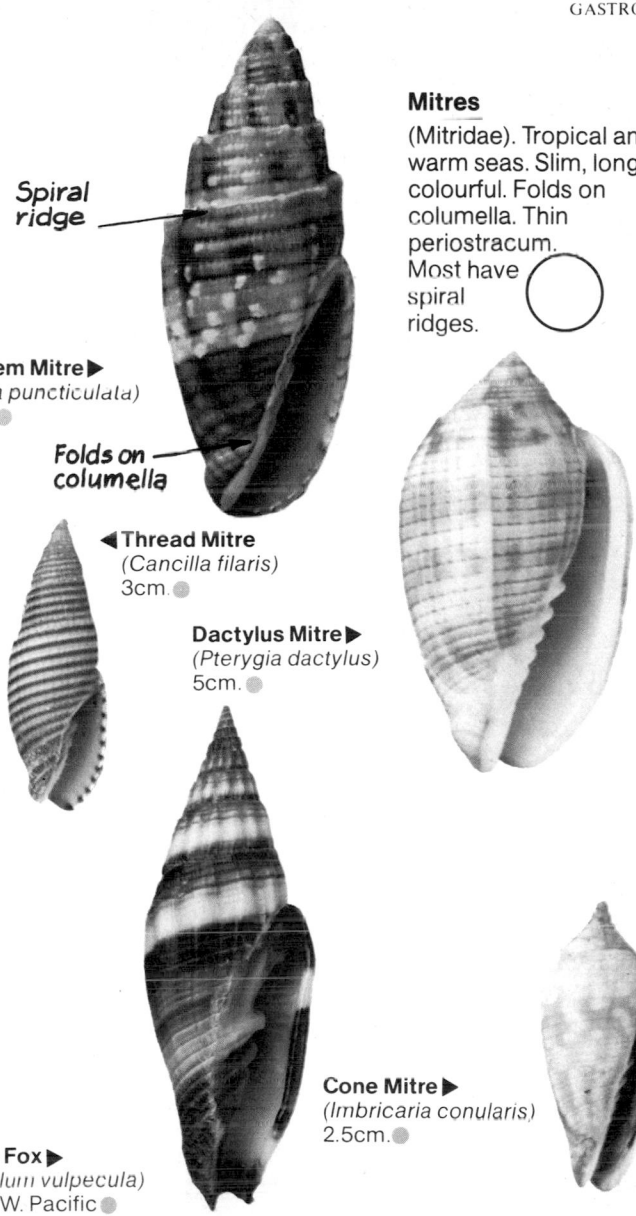

Mitres

(Mitridae). Tropical and warm seas. Slim, long and colourful. Folds on columella. Thin periostracum. Most have spiral ridges.

Diadem Mitre▶
(Mitra puncticulata)
6cm.

◀**Thread Mitre**
(Cancilla filaris)
3cm.

Dactylus Mitre▶
(Pterygia dactylus)
5cm.

Cone Mitre▶
(Imbricaria conularis)
2.5cm.

Little Fox▶
(Vexillum vulpecula)
7cm. W. Pacific

Margin Shells

(Marginellidae). Warm and tropical seas. Spire short or covered by body whorl. Usually 3-5 folds on columella. Thick outer lip. No periostracum. Smooth, shiny shells.

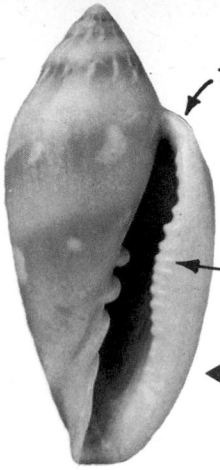

◀ **Desjardin's Margin**
(Marginella desjardini)
7cm. ●

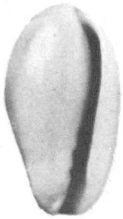

◀ **Orange Margin**
(Prunum oblonga)
2.5cm. ●

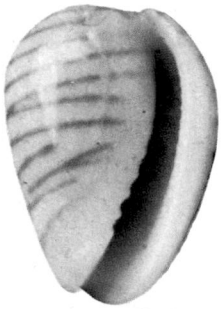

Striper Margin ▶
(Persicula cingula)
2cm. ●

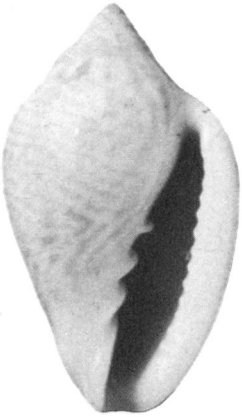

◀ **Loup Margin**
(Persicula phyrgia)
0.5cm. ●

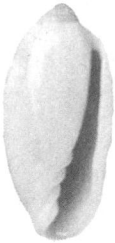

Philippine Margin ▶
(Volvarina philippinarium)
1.5cm. W. Pacific ●

▲ **Pink Margin**
(Marginella irrorata)
3cm. ●

Olives

(Olividae). Tropical and warm seas. Smooth, shiny shells. Short spire. Body whorl is almost whole length of shell. Long opening with small folds on inner lip.

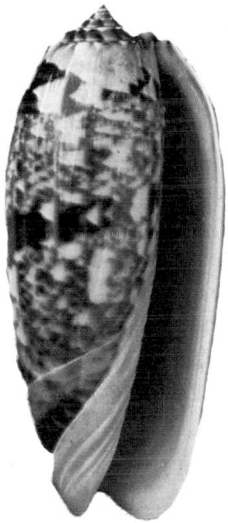

Tent Olive ▶
(Oliva porphyria)
15cm.

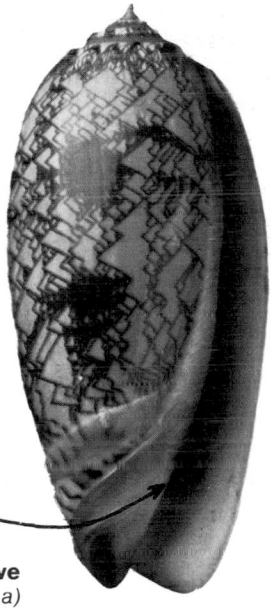

Folds on inner lip

◀ **Red Mouth Olive**
(Oliva mineacea)
10cm.

Fat Olive ▶
(Olivancillaria gibbosa)
5cm.

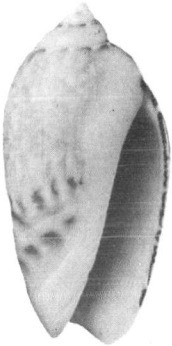

◀ **Lady Olive**
(Olivella dama)
2.5cm.

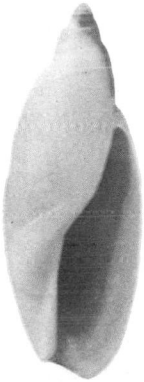

◀ **Long Ancilla**
(Amalda elongata)
5cm. N. Australia

Volutes (p. 32-33)

(Volutidae). Temperate, warm and tropical seas; especially in Australia. Shells mostly thick, shiny, heavy and colourful. Usually large protoconch, which is often smooth and rounded.

◀ **Cuming's Volute**
(Lyria cumingi)
3.5cm.

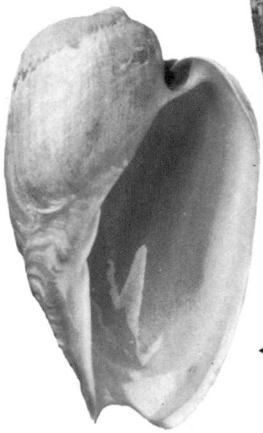

Hebrew Volute ▶
(Voluta ebraea)
15cm.

◀ **Algarve Volute**
(Cymbium olla)
13cm.

Imperial Volute ▶
(Cymbiola imperialis)
25cm. Philippines

Smooth protoconch

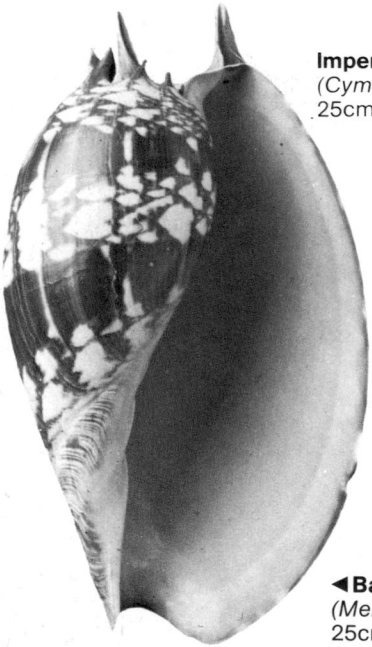

◀ **Baler Shell**
(Melo amphorus)
25cm. W. Pacific

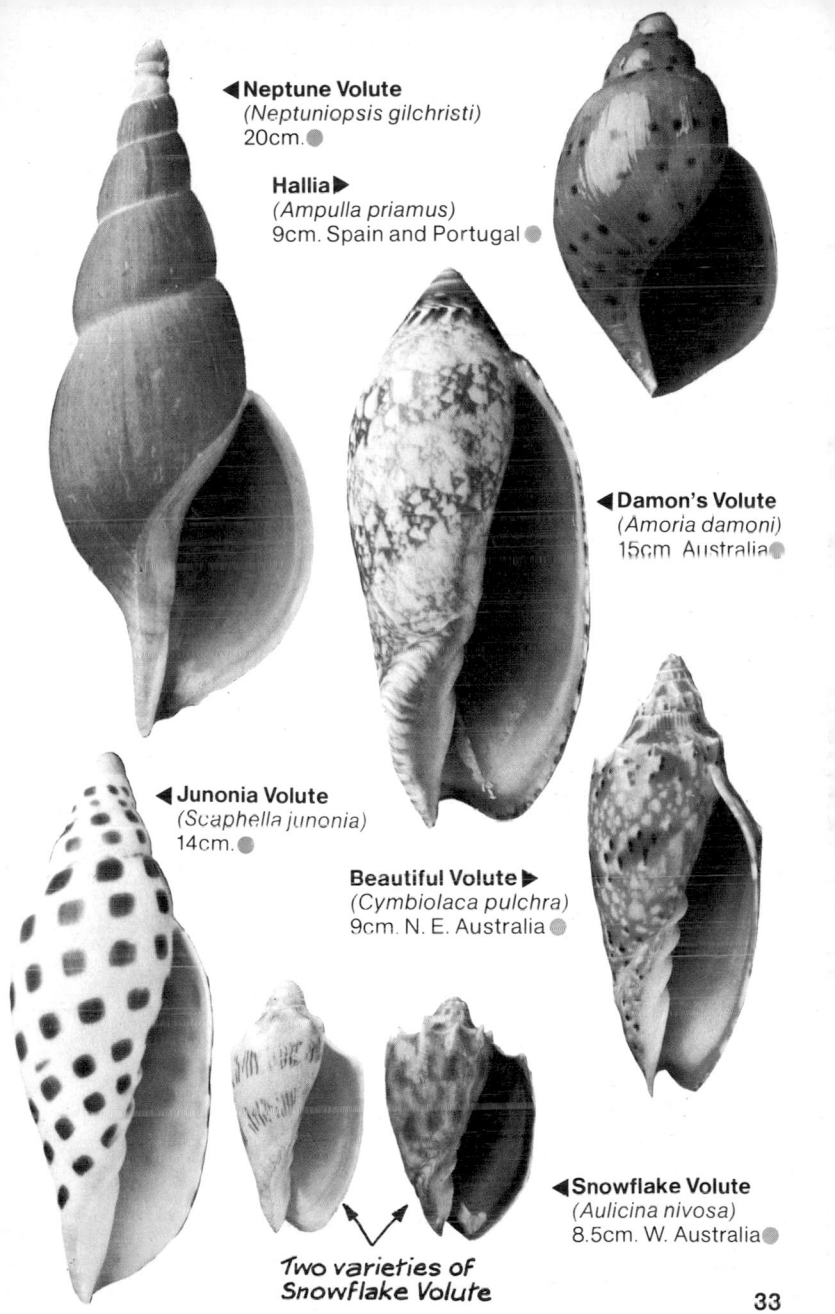
◀ Neptune Volute
(Neptuniopsis gilchristi)
20cm.
Hallia ▶
(Ampulla priamus)
9cm. Spain and Portugal
◀ Damon's Volute
(Amoria damoni)
15cm. Australia
◀ Junonia Volute
(Scaphella junonia)
14cm.
Beautiful Volute ▶
(Cymbiolaca pulchra)
9cm. N. E. Australia
◀ Snowflake Volute
(Aulicina nivosa)
8.5cm. W. Australia
Two varieties of
Snowflake Volute

◀ **Sieve Cowrie**
(Cypraea cribraria)
3.5cm.

Humpback Cowrie ▶
(Cypraea decipiens)
6cm. W. Australia

◀ **Atlantic Cowrie**
(Cypraea spurca)
3cm.

◀ **Little Deer Cowrie**
(Cypraea cervinetta)
9cm.

Cowries

(Cypraeidae). Tropical and warm seas. Body whorl forms the whole shell. Shiny, smooth shells with a row of "teeth" on both lips. About 180 species.

◀ **European Cowrie**
(Trivia monacha)
1.5cm.

Button Shells

(Eratoidae). Tropical and warm seas. Small shells similar to Cowries but with grooves across the back of shell. Many are microshells.

Radiant Button Shell ▶
(Trivia radians)
2cm.

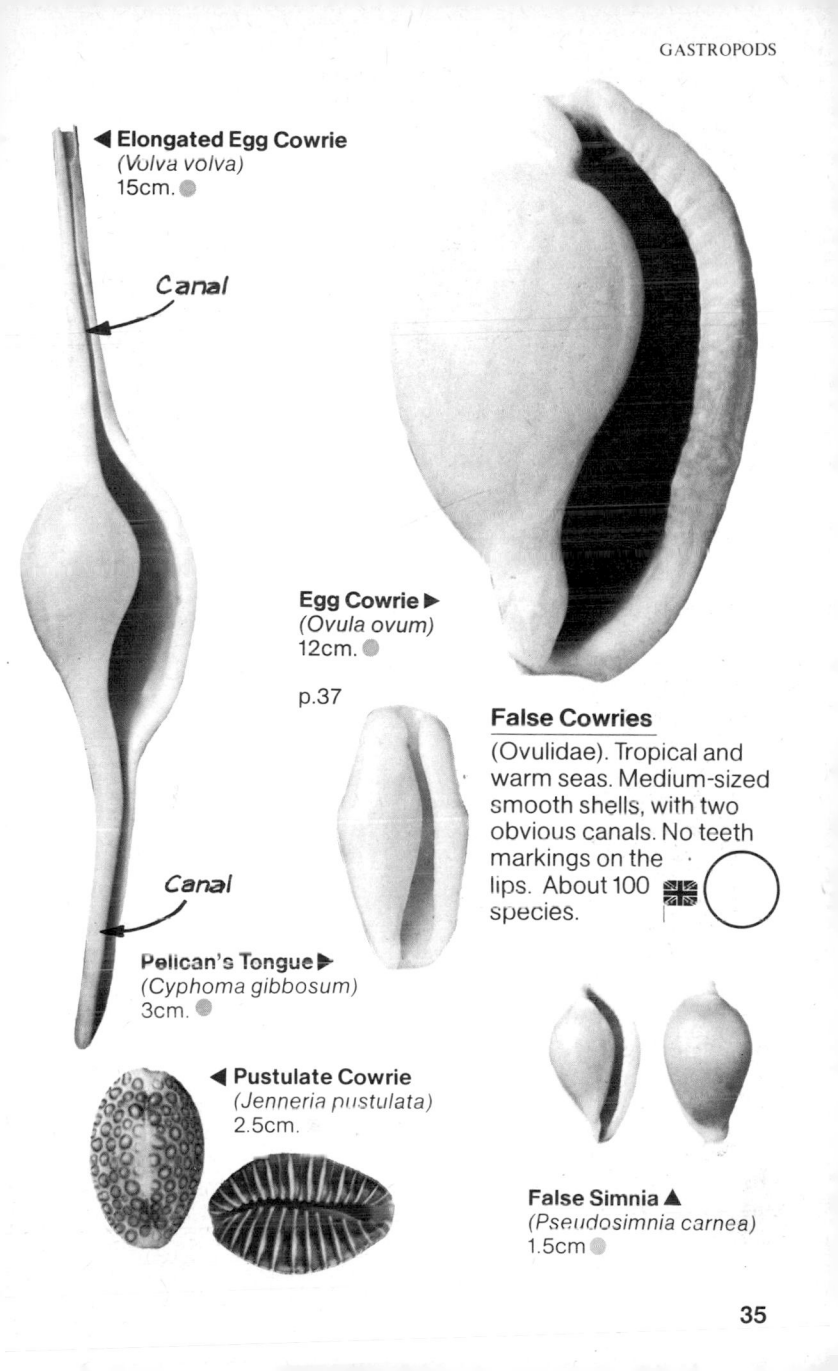

◀ **Elongated Egg Cowrie**
(Volva volva)
15cm.

Egg Cowrie ▶
(Ovula ovum)
12cm.

p.37

False Cowries

(Ovulidae). Tropical and warm seas. Medium-sized smooth shells, with two obvious canals. No teeth markings on the lips. About 100 species.

Pelican's Tongue ▶
(Cyphoma gibbosum)
3cm.

◀ **Pustulate Cowrie**
(Jenneria pustulata)
2.5cm.

False Simnia ▲
(Pseudosimnia carnea)
1.5cm

◀ **Rustic Dove Shell**
(Pyrene rustica)
2.5cm.

Dove Shells

(Pyrenidae). Warm and tropical seas. Strong, small, colourful shells. Often in large numbers in seaweed. Usually covered in lime or weed when alive.

(Strombina dorsata) ▶
3cm.

Bubble Shells

(Opisthobrachia). Tropical and warm seas. Thin, fragile shells. Thin outer lip. Sunken spire. Found in sand and mud.

Sunken spire

White Banded Bubble ▶
(Hydatina albocincta)
6cm.

Canoe Shell ▶
(Scaphander lignarius)
7cm

◀ **Pacific Bubble**
(Bulla ampulla)
6cm.

Nut Shells ▶

(Nuculidae). Worldwide. Small, strong shells with pearly interior. Many tiny hinge teeth. Equal valves.

◀ Nut Shell
(Nucula nucleus)
1.2cm.

◀ Ponderous Ark
(Noetia ponderosa)
6cm.

Ark Shells

(Arcidae). Worldwide. Straight hinge with many teeth fitting closely together. Equal valves.

Turkey Wing ▶
(Arca zebra)
9cm.

Hinge teeth

Hairy Ark ▲
(Barbatia barbatia)
6cm.

Dog Cockles/Bitter Sweets ▶

(Glycymerididae). Worldwide. Round, heavy shells with saw-like edges. Two groups of hinge teeth parallel to edge of shell.

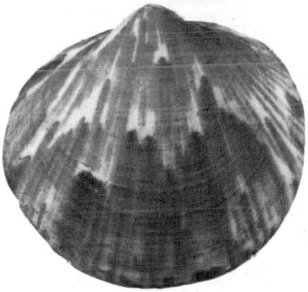

Bitter Sweet ▲
(Petunculus formosus)
9cm.

Horse Mussel ▶
(Modiolus modiolus)
22cm.

Blue Mussel ▲
(Mytilus edulis)
12cm.

◀ Date Mussel
(Lithophaga lithophaga)
7cm.

Mussels

(Mytilidae). Worldwide. Blue or brown. Live attached to rocks by threads. Valves are equal size and do not have teeth. Edible. Very common.

◀ Yellow Mussel
(Brachidontes citrinus)
5cm.

▼ Radiant Cardita
(Cardita radians)
4.5cm.

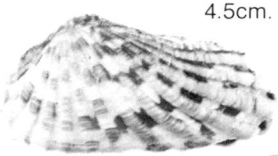

European Cardita ▶
(Cardita calyculata)
2.5cm.

◀ Carditas

(Carditidae). Worldwide. Small, often elongated, shells with distinct ribs. Equal valves. One major hinge tooth. Under stones in shallow water.

Saw-like edge

Cockles

(Cardidae). Worldwide. Heart-shaped shell. Most have strong ribs with saw-like edges. Two central teeth on hinge, and usually one or two teeth on each side of the hinge.

◀**China Cockle**
(Trachycardium egmontianum)
4cm.

Egg Cockle▶
(Laevicardium laevigatum)
4cm.

◀**Long Giant Clam**
(Tridacna elongata)
32cm.

Giant Clams

(Tridacnidae). Tropical areas of Indo-Pacific. Large, thick, heavy shells. Gap near the hinge through which the mollusc anchors itself. Six species.

Gap

Fluted Giant Clam▼
(Tridacna squamosa)
40cm.

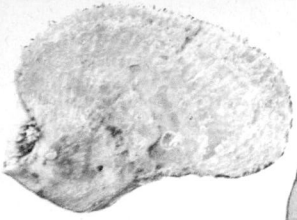

Flat Oyster▲
(Isognomon isognomon)
12cm.

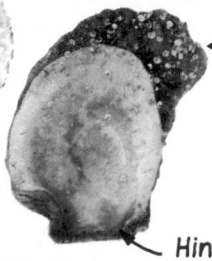

◀Hammer Oysters

(Isognominidae). Tropical parts of Atlantic and Pacific. Flat shells with a long, straight row of hinge teeth.

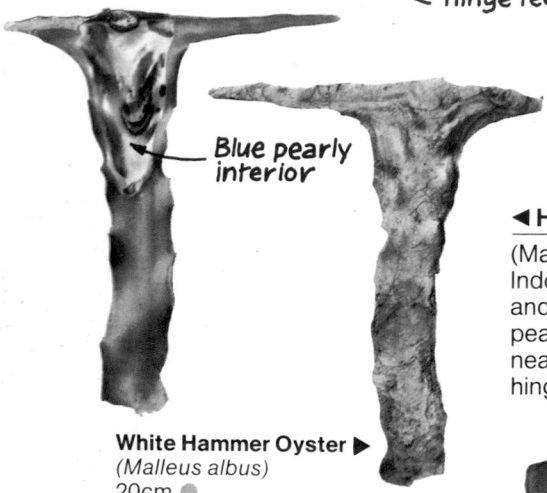

◀ Hammer Oysters

(Malleidae). Tropical Indo-Pacific. Wide base and narrow body. Blue pearly interior near the hinge.

White Hammer Oyster ▶
(Malleus albus)
20cm.

Pearl Oyster ▶
(Pinctada margaritifera)
18cm.

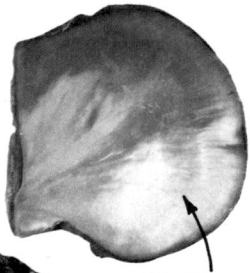

Pearl Oysters

(Pteriidae). Tropical and warm seas. Outside is scaly, inside is mother-of-pearl. Wing-like extensions on hinge.

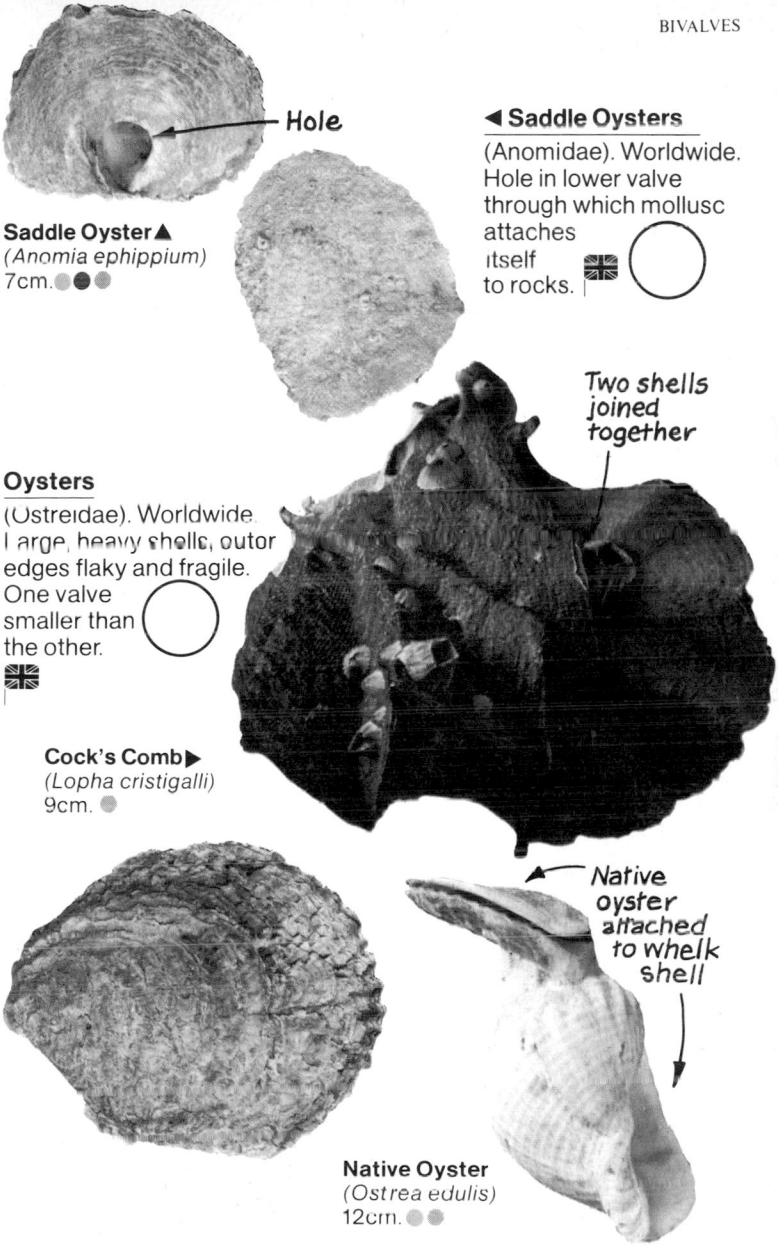

Saddle Oyster▲
(Anomia ephippium)
7cm.

◀ Saddle Oysters
(Anomidae). Worldwide. Hole in lower valve through which mollusc attaches itself to rocks.

Oysters
(Ostreidae). Worldwide. Large, heavy shells, outer edges flaky and fragile. One valve smaller than the other.

Cock's Comb▶
(Lopha cristigalli)
9cm.

Native Oyster
(Ostrea edulis)
12cm.

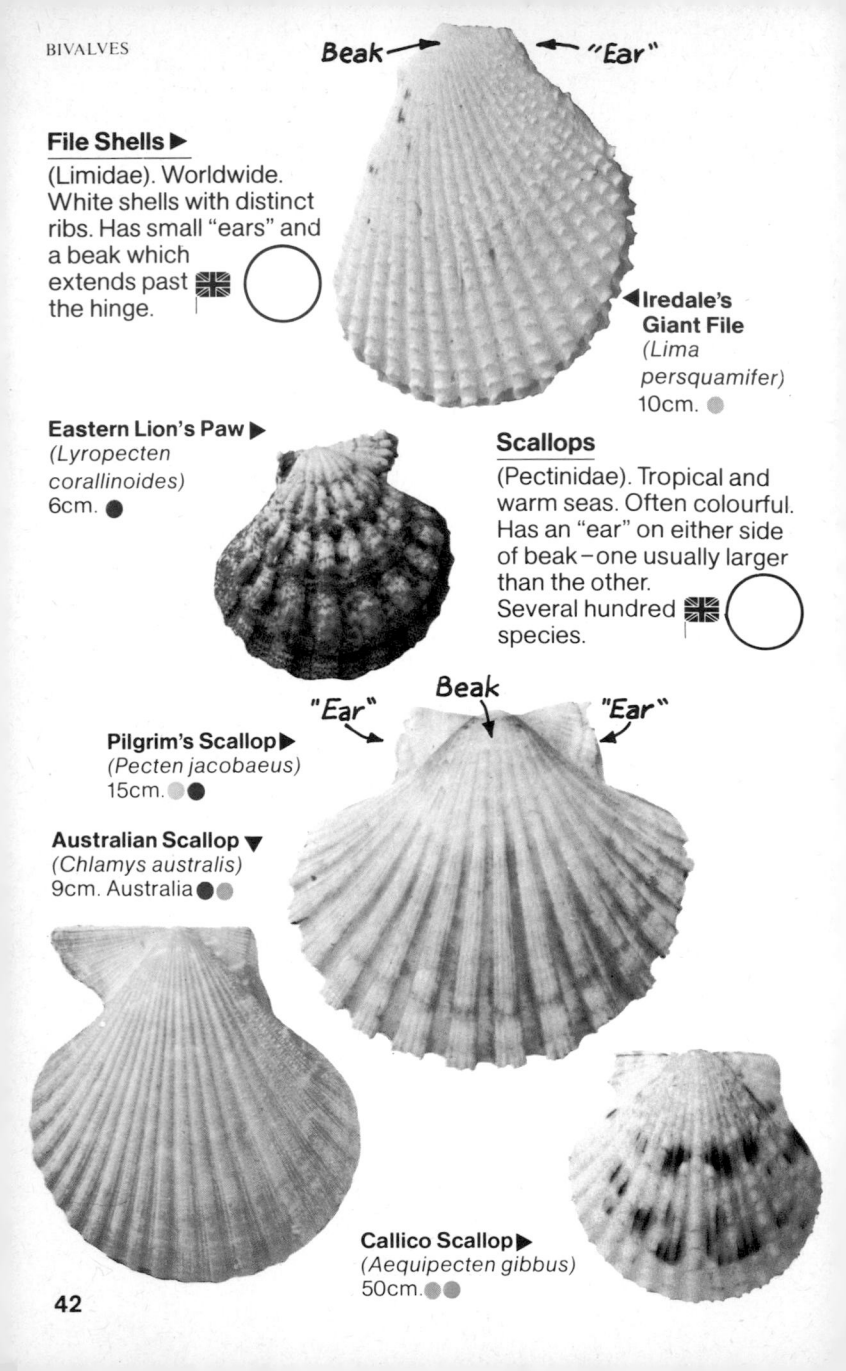

File Shells ▶

(Limidae). Worldwide. White shells with distinct ribs. Has small "ears" and a beak which extends past the hinge.

◀Iredale's Giant File
(Lima persquamifer)
10cm.

Eastern Lion's Paw ▶
(Lyropecten corallinoides)
6cm.

Scallops

(Pectinidae). Tropical and warm seas. Often colourful. Has an "ear" on either side of beak – one usually larger than the other. Several hundred species.

Pilgrim's Scallop ▶
(Pecten jacobaeus)
15cm.

Australian Scallop ▼
(Chlamys australis)
9cm. Australia

Callico Scallop ▶
(Aequipecten gibbus)
50cm.

◀ Thorny Oysters

(Spondylidae). Tropical and warm seas. Attaches itself to solid objects. Often has long or short spines.

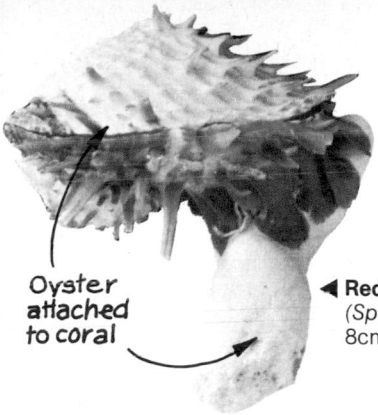

◀ **Red Thorny Oyster**
(Spondylus coccineus)
8cm. Philippines

Jewel Boxes ▶

(Chamidae). Tropical seas. Beak usually strongly curved. Shape varies. Usually covered in seaweed or dead coral.

Leaf Chama ▶
(Chama lazarus)
15cm.

Venus Clams

(Veneriidae). Worldwide. Strong, heavy shells. Small but long hinge teeth. Muscle scars on inside of shell.

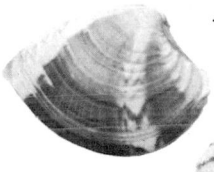

◀ **Kellet's Venus**
(Chione kelletia)
4cm.

Tent Venus ▶
(Lioconcha castrenis)
4.5cm.

Lamellate Venus ▶
(Antigonia lamellaris)
4.5cm. W. Pacific

◀**Panama Coquina**
(Donax panamensis)
4cm.

Wedge Shells

(Donacidae). Worldwide. Small, shiny, wedge-shaped shell with saw-like edge. Both valves same size.

◀**Great False Coquina**
(Iphigenia brasiliensis)
7cm.

Tellins

(Tellinidae). Worldwide. Flat, thin, usually delicate shell. Stripes of colour on shell. Valves often unequal.

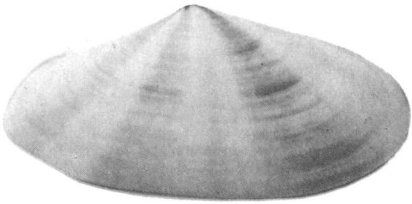

Sunrise Shell ▲
(Tellina radiata)
6cm.

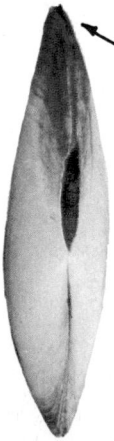

◀**Flat Tellin**
(Tellina planata)
6cm.

Sunset Shells ▶

(Psammobiidae). Worldwide. Thin, flat shells. Similar to Tellins, but more symmetrical. Equal valves which have a gap at each end when closed.

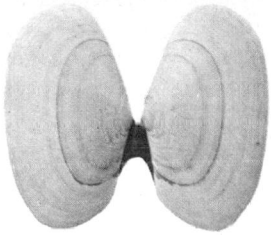

Stanger's Sanguin ▲
(Gari stangeri)
6cm. New Zealand ●

Trough Shells

(Mactridae). Worldwide. Heavy and white or fragile and thin shells. Pale blue or yellow. Triangular dent in hinge.

Violet Surf Clam ▲
(Mactra violacea)
8cm. ●

◀ Australian Surf Clam
(Mactra australis)
5cm. N. Australia ●

Beak

Lucines

(Lucinidae). Worldwide. Thin, round shells. Most are white. Small but distinct beak.

Beak

Orb Lucine ▲
(Codakia orbicularis)
8cm. ●

Buttercup Lucine ▶
(Anodonta alba)
5cm. ● ●

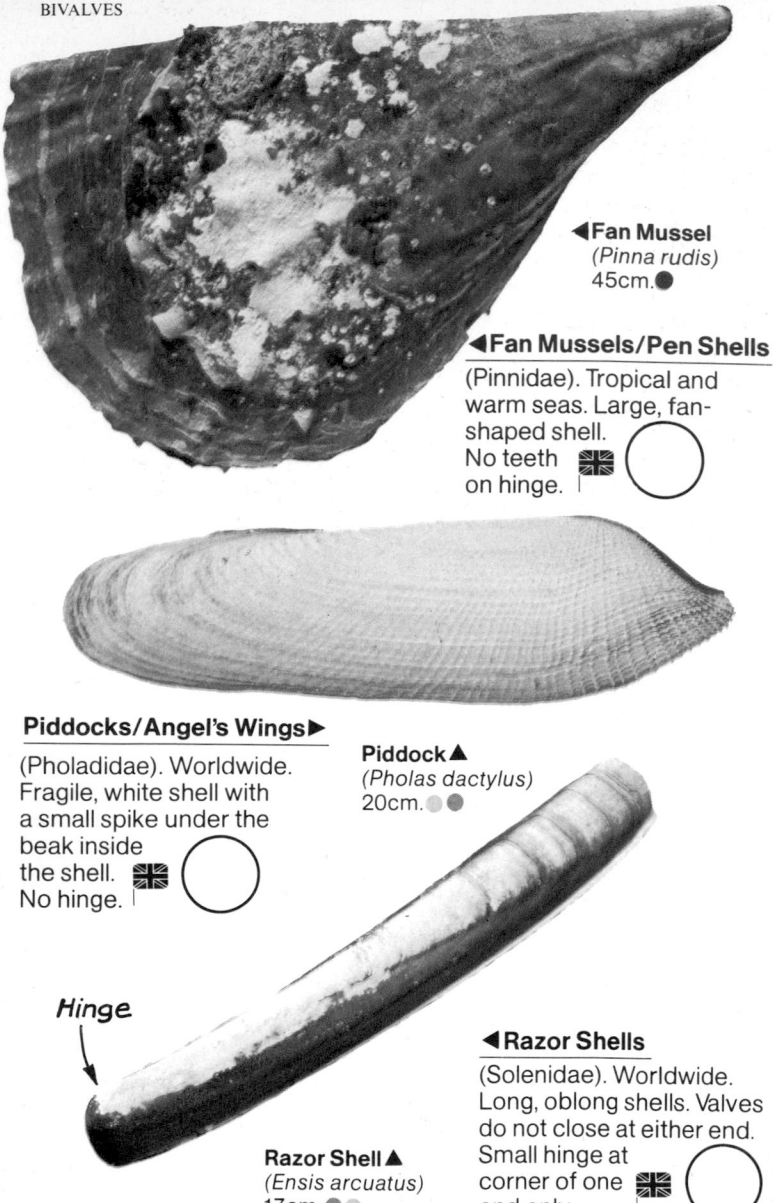

◀**Fan Mussel**
(Pinna rudis)
45cm.●

◀**Fan Mussels/Pen Shells**

(Pinnidae). Tropical and warm seas. Large, fan-shaped shell. No teeth on hinge.

Piddocks/Angel's Wings▶

(Pholadidae). Worldwide. Fragile, white shell with a small spike under the beak inside the shell. No hinge.

Piddock▲
(Pholas dactylus)
20cm.●●

◀**Razor Shells**

(Solenidae). Worldwide. Long, oblong shells. Valves do not close at either end. Small hinge at corner of one end only.

Razor Shell▲
(Ensis arcuatus)
17cm.●●

Chitons

(Amphineura). Worldwide. All species of this class have a shell made up of eight overlapping plates with a leathery girdle. Shell is flexible and smooth or spiny. Difficult to preserve.

▲ **Spiny Chiton**
(Acanthopleura spinosa)
15cm. N. Australia

◀ **Lined Chiton**
(Ionicella lineata)
4cm

Tusk Shells

(Scaphopoda). Worldwide. Long shells open at both ends. Buried in mud in deep water. Often washed up on beaches after storms. Over 300 species.

◀ **Elephant Tooth**
(Dentalium elephantium)
9cm.

◀ **Rosy Tooth**
(Dentalium rubescens)
3.5cm.

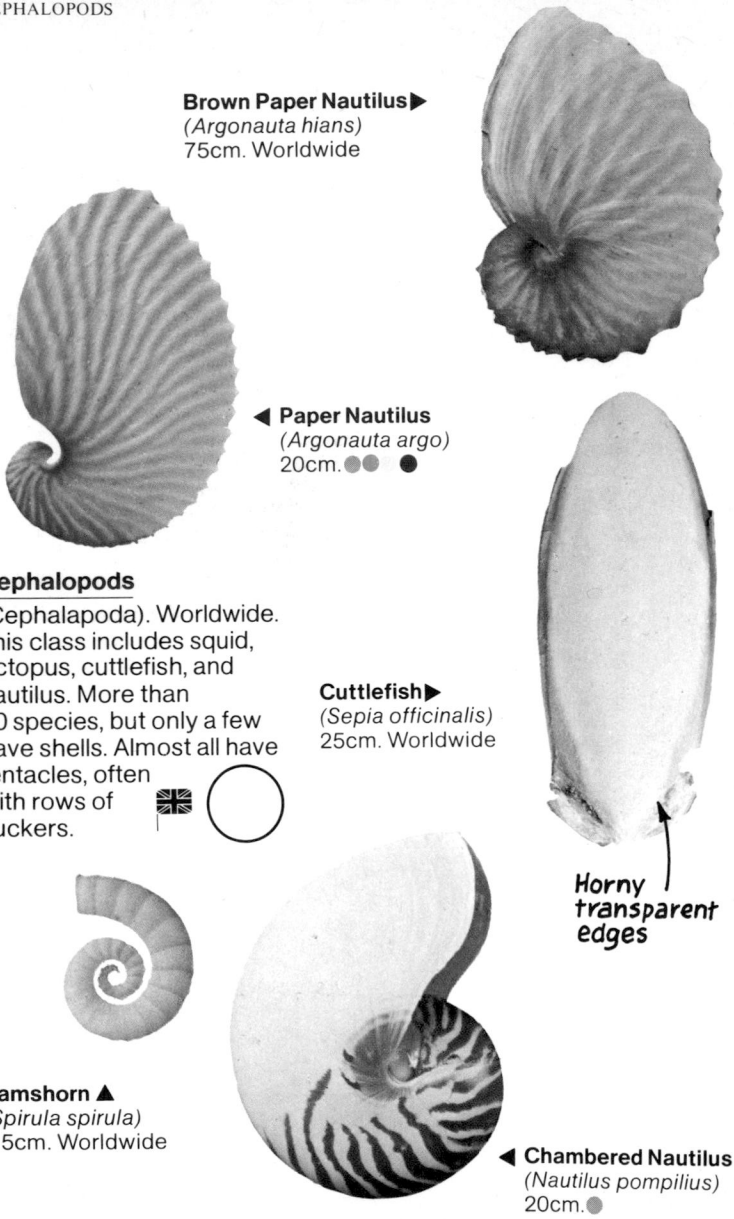

Brown Paper Nautilus▶
(Argonauta hians)
75cm. Worldwide

◀ **Paper Nautilus**
(Argonauta argo)
20cm.

Cephalopods

(Cephalapoda). Worldwide. This class includes squid, octopus, cuttlefish, and nautilus. More than 50 species, but only a few have shells. Almost all have tentacles, often with rows of suckers.

Cuttlefish▶
(Sepia officinalis)
25cm. Worldwide

Ramshorn ▲
(Spirula spirula)
3.5cm. Worldwide

◀ **Chambered Nautilus**
(Nautilus pompilius)
20cm.

Parts of a shell

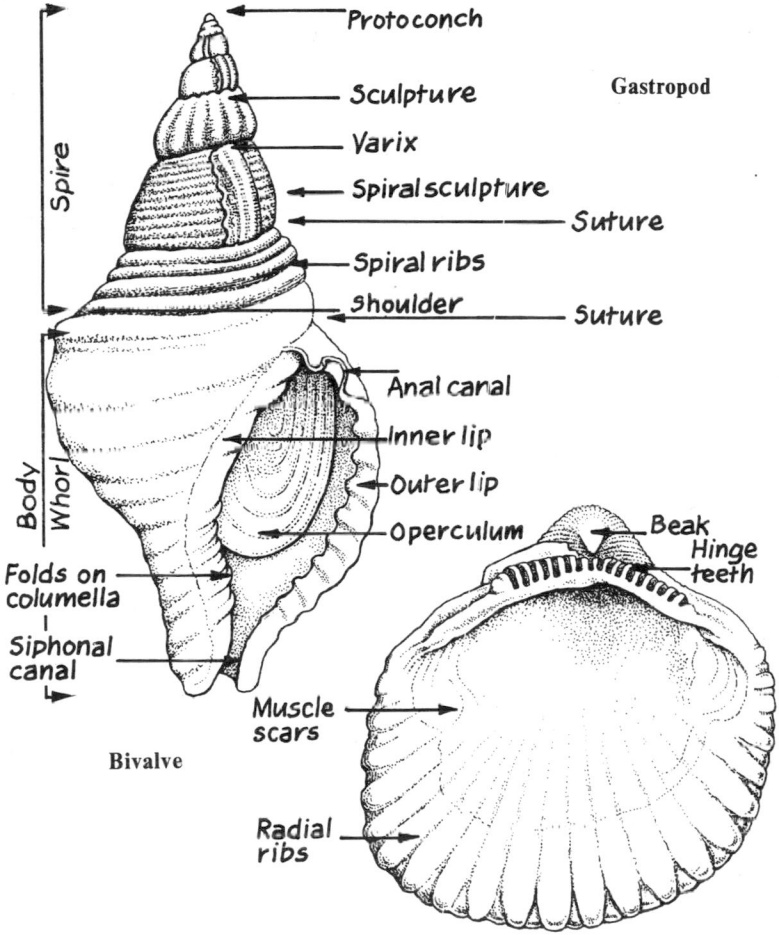

In the field guide part of the book there is a description of each shell family. A number of species make up a family, so any features in common have been described to help you identify the family.

Above are drawings of a gastropod and a bivalve showing their different features and the special words used to name them.

If there are any words you don't understand or if you need further explanation, turn to the Glossary on page 60.

How shells grow

A shell is a mollusc's covering for its soft body and is a protection against its enemies. It is formed from a thin layer called a mantle, which covers the body of the mollusc. The mantle secretes a limy substance which hardens on contact with air or water to form a shell.

The shell is made up of three layers: the periostracum, the pigmented layer and calcium layer. The periostracum is a very thin layer which protects the shell and hides its natural colour. Shells found on the beach are usually colourful because the periostracum has been rubbed away while the shell was drifting in the sea. Some shells, like cowries, do not have a periostracum.

The calcium layer is fine and smooth, and is sometimes mother-of-pearl. The pigmented layer is the colourful part of the shell.

A magnified cross-section of a shell

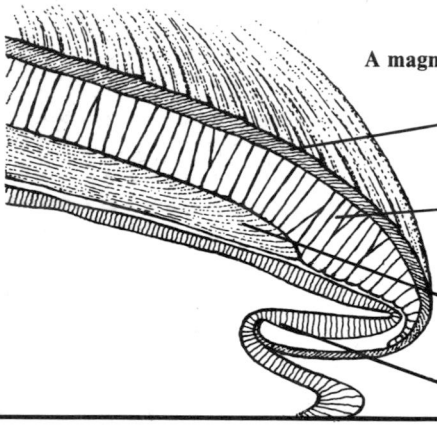

Shell rings

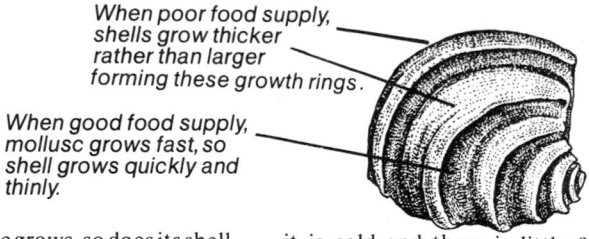

As a mollusc grows, so does its shell. Shells in tropical seas are usually bigger, more colourful, thinner and lighter than shells of the same family that live in colder waters.

Molluscs grow faster when there is a plentiful food supply than when it is cold and there is little food. Shells grow at a fairly steady rate, but if there is not enough food the mollusc does not. On bivalves you can see a growth pattern that is similar to the annual growth rings seen in tree trunks.

Biology of a mollusc

A mollusc's body is soft and has no skeleton. The shell is the animal's protection into which it can withdraw when in danger. The body is usually divided into the head, which consists of a mouth and nerve centre, a muscular foot, and the visceral mass, which contains its organs, like the heart and digestive system. The body is completely surrounded by the mantle, from which the shell is formed.

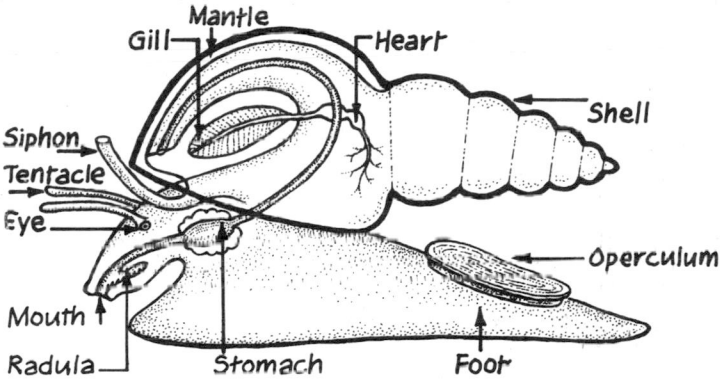

A **gastropod** has a coiled shell with an opening which relates to its body size. On its foot it often has an operculum which seals the shell opening when the animal is inside. On its head are two pairs of tentacles; one pair contains the sense organs, and the other usually has eyes at either the top or the bottom. It has a radula or "tongue", which is a horny strip with tiny teeth, used to scrape at either seaweed, or animals (dead or living). It lays live young or eggs that hatch into miniature snails or free-swimming larvae called "veligers" (see page 52).

A **bivalve** has two shells which are hinged together with little "teeth" which interlock. The shells are kept closed by a pair of strong muscles and opened by a rubbery ligament. The muscles are visible as scars on the inside of the shells. Some bivalves live attached to rocks and others burrow in sand, rock or mud. Bivalves breathe and food by drawing water into the gills. The gills absorb oxygen and collect tiny particles of animal and vegetable matter that are passed into the mouth. Bivalves lay eggs that hatch into free-swimming veligers.

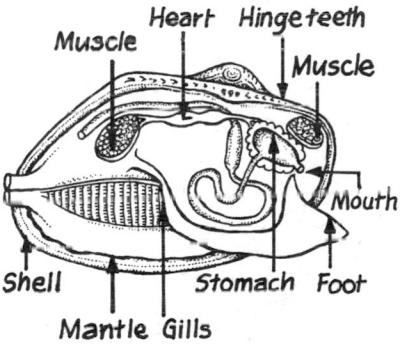

Life cycle of a mollusc

Some species can be found all over the world, while others live only in certain small areas of the world. One of the reasons for this is that some start life in their proper habitat and never move far from it, while others have a time of free-floating in the sea. These could be carried miles from where they were hatched, before they sink to the bottom, where they may or may not find a suitable habitat.

Some molluscs are laid as eggs and hatch into tiny shelled "crawlers," and some are born as "crawlers." Others are laid as eggs and hatch into "veligers." A veliger is free-swimming and has the beginning of a shell. It lives in the sea with the tiny animals and plants called plankton.

Thousands of the tiny veligers are hatched from hundreds of egg capsules. So many are laid because hundreds are eaten by fish and other animals, and others never find a suitable habitat. In fact only a few ever live to become adults.

The tiny shelled "crawlers" are born into their own habitat, so fewer need to be laid to make sure that some survive.

This shows the different stages in the life of a gastropod called a Murex.

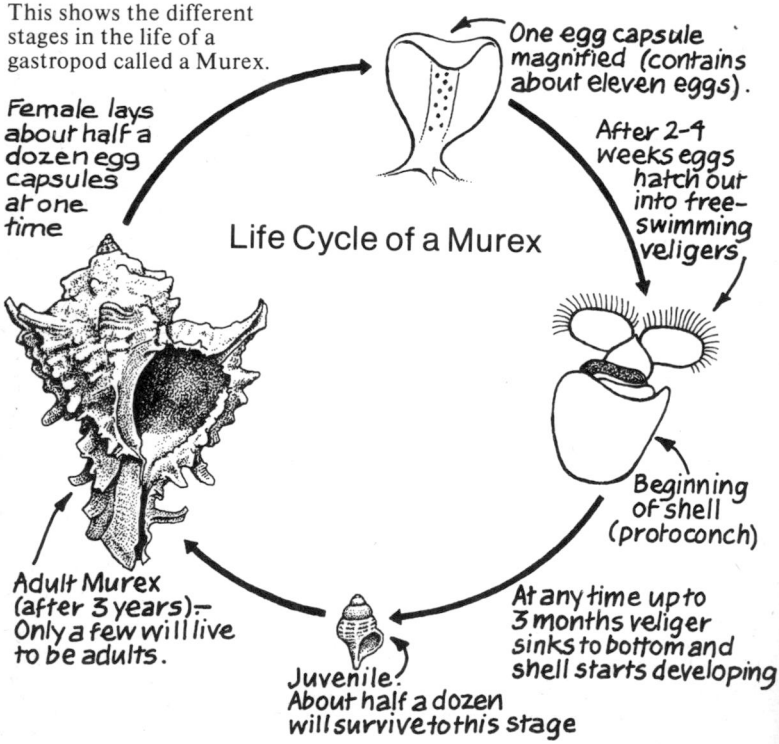

How a mollusc moves

Although molluscs do not have legs to walk about on, they have a muscular foot. They move either to find a better food supply or to escape from their enemies.

Gastropods usually move by a rippling movement of the foot; some lighter species swim this way.

Some bivalves expand and contract their foot to move through mud and sand. Others clap their shells together and by shooting water out from between their shells, move forwards or backwards.

A gastropod

A Gastropod has three contraction waves that move from the back of the foot to the front.

2. Wave is set into motion.

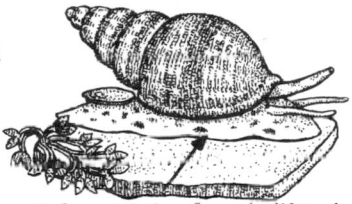

1. Part of the foot is lifted.

3. Foot moves forward

A bivalve

The file shell claps its two shells together to move forward.

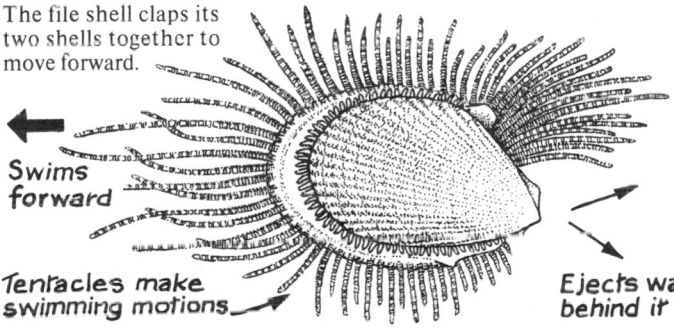

Where shells live . . .

Molluscs have adapted to particular habitats which give them the best possible chance of survival, where they can find food, protection from their enemies, and where they can breed successfully. Here are some examples of different habitats and the type of shells you find in them.

Sandy shore

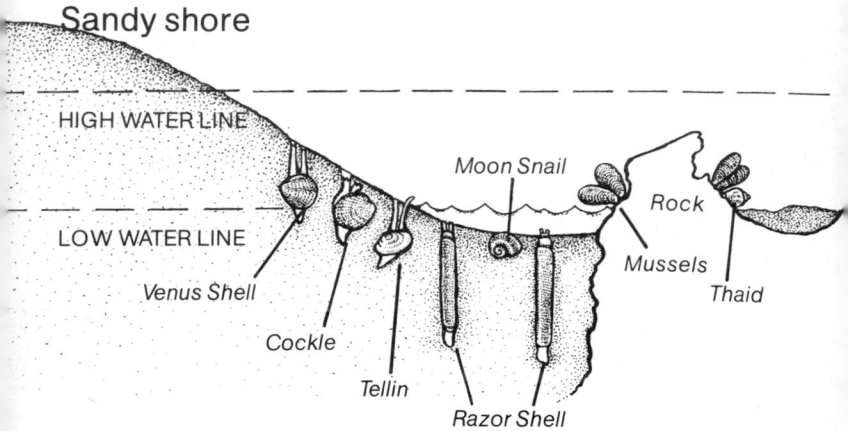

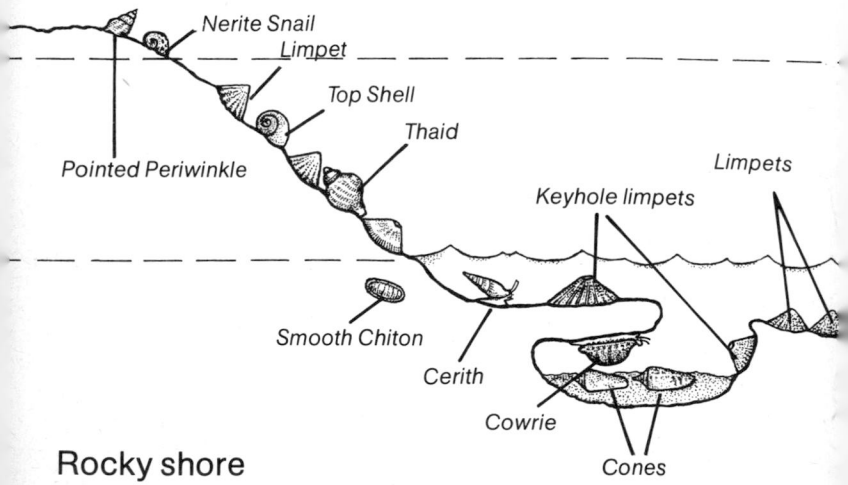

Rocky shore

. . . rocky and sandy shores

Shells which are not related often have similar shapes because they live in the same kinds of habitats. For instance, mud-living species (see next page) may have side spines or thin spires to steady themselves. Shells attached to rocks are usually smooth and broad; rocky-bottomed dwellers have heavy, knobbly shells. In coral, (see next page) frilly spines can act as camouflage.

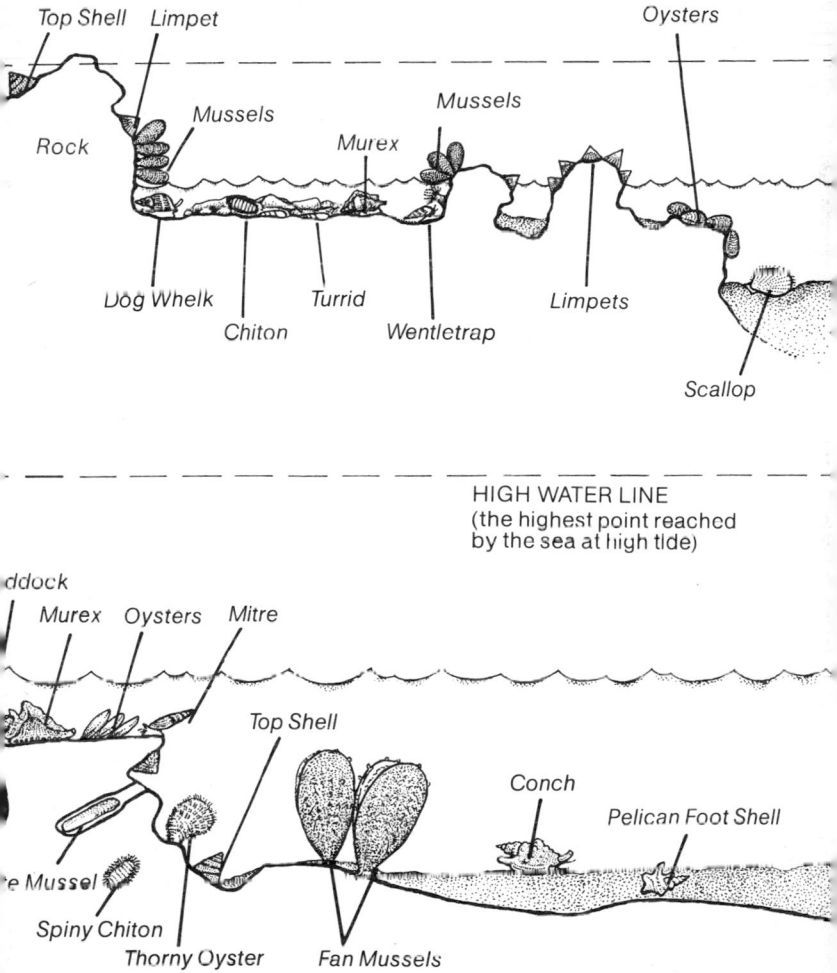

Muddy shore

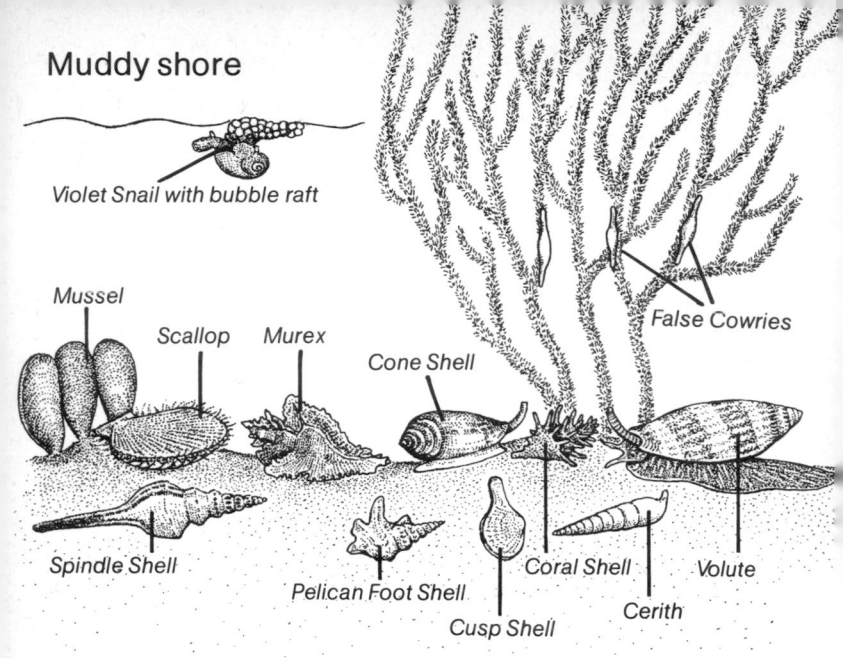

Coral

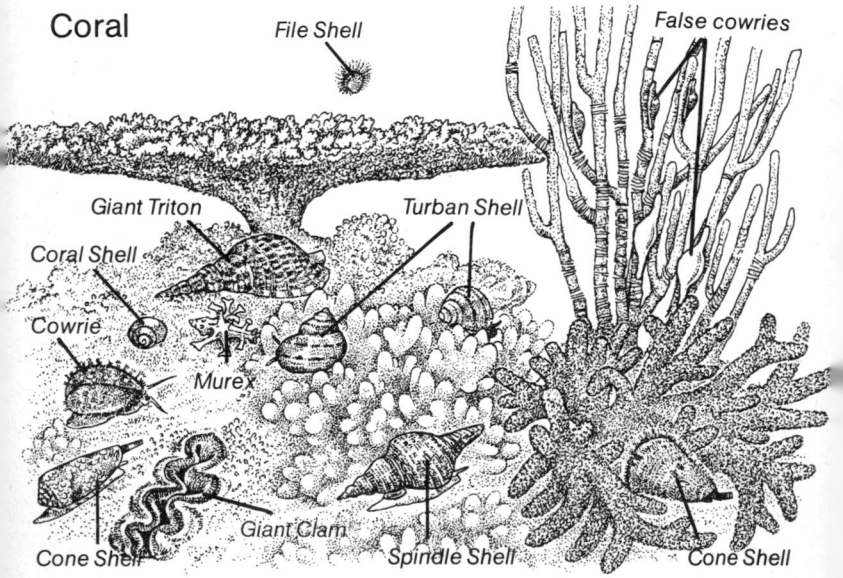

Collecting shells

What to take
You need a plastic bucket, bags or jam jars to put your shells in, and a sieve to sieve sand with. Tie string round them so you can hang them round your neck and keep your hands free for turning rocks and picking up shells. It's a good idea to make notes about what you find, so take a notebook and pencil wrapped in a plastic bag.

Where to look
Shells can be found on most beaches but sometimes they are hard to see. On the previous pages you can find out what type of shells to expect on a particular shore.

A good time to start looking is at low tide. You can start at the high water line, and look among the debris washed up there. Turn seaweed over as shells may still be clinging to it. Look for shells as you walk down to the sea and as the tide comes in, walk back and collect any shells that the sea throws up.

After a storm the beach is always worth searching. You should be able to find some quite large shells. Many will be damaged but by looking carefully you may find some good specimens.

On sandy beaches look out for microshells. These are tiny, but are no less interesting than the larger ones and can easily be missed. Sieve the sand and see what you find.

On rocky shores it is best to collect at low tide. Look in rock pools and tiny crevices. Turn small rocks over to see what is underneath, but remember to put them back where you found them.

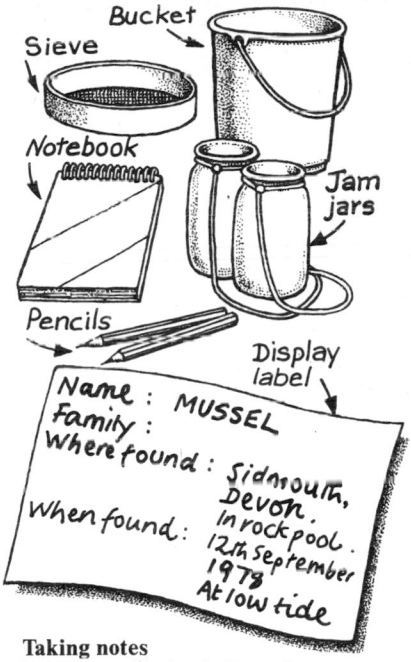

Taking notes
When you find a shell, make a note of its name, where and when you found it. If you don't know the name, look it up when you get home. Without this information a shell is just a shell, but with it, the shell becomes a scientific specimen. When you get home you can put all this information on a display label or index card.

Before setting off down the beach to collect shells take note of the times of the tides to make sure that you don't get stranded.

Cleaning and storing shells

Cleaning shells

If a shell is covered in weed or barnacles, or still has its periostracum, (see page 50) you can clean it. Put it in an equal mixture of warm water and household bleach (wear rubber gloves when mixing.) Leave it overnight. In the morning brush the shell very carefully with a toothbrush. Don't polish or varnish shells. If they look dull and colourless, wipe them over with a cloth soaked in light oil or medicinal paraffin.

If you want to keep the periostracum, don't leave the shell in the bleach for longer than ten minutes. Use the toothbrush very lightly, as the periostracum tends to flake off when dry.

Never put the operculum (see page 51) in bleach because it will dissolve.

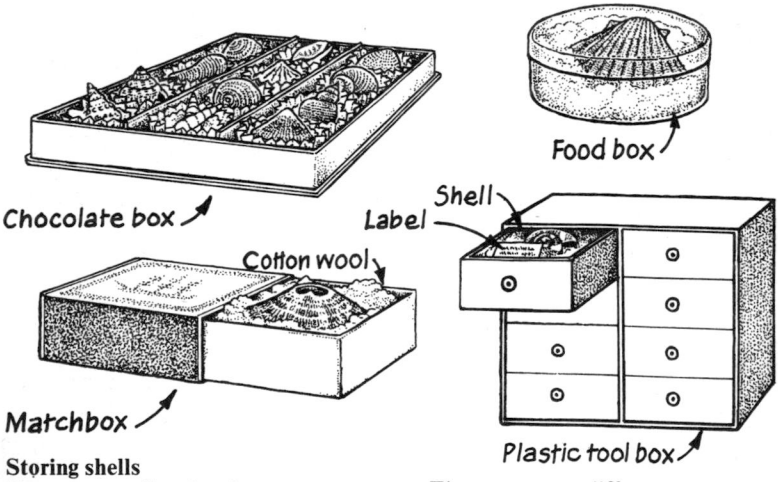

Storing shells

Keep your collection in some sort of order. Try to keep the families together, and then store them either by locality or in date order. Put the scientific information on a card and store it with the shell.

Always store shells away from sunlight or they will fade, become dried out and fragile.

There are many different ways of storing shells. It is possible to buy many-drawered cabinets for shells, but you can also put them separately in plastic bags and store them tidily in a drawer or use matchboxes, sweet tins, plastic food containers, chocolate boxes or plastic tool boxes.

Books to read

The Encyclopedia of Shells. S. Peter Dance (Blandford)
The Hamlyn Guide to Shells of the World. A.P. H. Oliver (Hamlyn)
Identification of British Mollusca. Gordon Beedham (Hulton Educational Publications)
Seashells. S. Peter Dance (Hamlyn)
Seashells of the British and European Coasts. J. Arrecgros (Spectrum Colour Books)
A Field-guide to Shells of the Atlantic and Gulf Coasts. Percy A. Morris (Peterson Field Guide Series)
Shells of the World. A. P. H. Oliver (Hamlyn)
What Shell is that? Neville Coleman (Hamlyn)
A good Italian shell magazine, in English, called *La Conchiglia* is available from The Editor, La Conchiglia, Via C Frederici 1, 00147 Rome, Italy.

Useful addresses

If you write to these shell clubs they should be able to give you information on shells in their areas.
The Secretary, *The British Shell Collectors' Club,* c/o 125 Lonsdale Drive, Rainham, Kent.
The Secretary, *Hawaiian Malacological Society,* PO Box 10391, Honolulu, Hawaii 96916, USA.
Australia has a number of local shell clubs. The *Keppel Bay Shell Club* produces a magazine called Keppel Bay Tidings. Write to the Secretary, PO Box 264, Yeppoon, Queensland 4703, Australia.
For a directory of the many shell clubs in America write to Tom Rice, Sea and Shore Publications, PO Box 33, Port Gamble, Washington 98354, USA.

Tips on collecting

When your friends go on holiday to other parts of the country or to other countries ask them to collect shells for you. You can then see how species vary from area to area. You can also arrange to swap shells with your friends when you get back from holiday.

When you are at the seaside ask the fishermen to keep shells that get tangled up in their nets for you.

Do not take live specimens of shells, however beautiful they might look. Some species around the world are now very rare because so many have been collected.

When you have collected shells from the seaside and want to know more about a particular family, or about shells in general, visit your local museum and ask to see their shell collection; most museums have one.

Many museums have space to display only a part of their collection. If there is a particular shell family you want to see, ask the museum staff. They will probably be helpful if they know that you are interested.

Glossary

Algae - water plants eg seaweed.
Aperture - opening in gastropod shell (see page 49).
Beak - earliest formed part of the bivalve shell (see page 49).
Bivalve - mollusc with two shells hinged together.
Body whorl - the last and largest coil of a gastropod shell.
Columella - central pillar at the opening of a gastropod shell (see page 49).
Crawlers - young molluscs that have a shell when they hatch from the egg.
Ear - small flat pieces on a bivalve on either side of the hinge (see page 49).
Gastropod - mollusc with a single shell which is usually coiled.
Habitat - a particular place where animals and plants live.
Hinge - the area where the two halves of bivalves join and where the ligament and teeth are situated.
Hinge teeth - interlocking device which keeps the two shells of the bivalve together (see pages 49 and 51).
Juvenile - a young mollusc.
Ligament - elastic material which opens the two shells of a bivalve when the muscles are relaxed.
Lip - outer edge of the opening of a gastropod shell.
Mantle - fold of "skin" which covers the mollusc's body (see pages 50 and 51).
Microshells - very small species of shells.
Muscle scars - marks on the inside of a bivalve where the muscles, which pull the shells together, were attached (see page 51).
Operculum - horny material on the gastropod foot that seals the shell opening when the animal is inside (see page 51).
Periostracum - a thin layer of horny material that protects the shell and usually hides its natural colour (see page 50).
Protoconch - the first formed whorl of a gastropod shell (see pages 49 and 52).
Sculpture - a raised pattern on a shell.
Radula - a horny "tongue" with tiny teeth, used for scraping at algae or animals (dead or alive).
Shoulder - an angular lump or ridge on the side of the body whorl.
Siphonal canal - a channel at the bottom of the gastropod shell opening (see page 49).
Species - shells that breed together and almost always look alike (see page 4).
Spines - spikes growing out from a shell.
Spire - part of the gastropod shell above the body whorl.
Suture - the place where two whorls join (see page 49).
Valve - one half of a bivalve shell.
Varix (plural: varices) - a thickened part of a shell, which was formed when there was a pause in the shell's growth.
Veliger - a free-swimming stage of a mollusc, before it becomes an adult (see page 52).
Whorl - one complete coil of a gastropod shell.

Scorecard

When you find a shell, write the date when it was found on the scorecard, and check your score. Shells with flags beside them are found in Britain, and the higher the score the rarer the shell. You can also tick off and score for the other species that are not found in Britain if you see them in museums or find them in shell shops.

	Score	Date seen
Ark Shells	10	
Augers	25	
Bubble Shells	10	
Button Shells	10	
Carditas	25	
Carrier shells	25	
Cephalopods	15	
Chitons	10	
Cockles	5	
Cone Shells	25	
Coral Snails	25	
Cowries	25	
Crown Conches	25	
Dog Cockles	10	
Dog Whelks	5	
Dove Shells	25	
False Cowries	20	
False Tritons	25	
Fan Mussels	25	
Fig Shells	25	
File Shells	15	

	Score	Date seen
Frog Shells	25	
Giant Clams	25	
Hairy Tritons	25	
Hammer Oysters	25	
Harp Shells	25	
Helmet Shells	25	
Hoof Shells	25	
Horn Shells	10	
Jewel Boxes	25	
Keyhole Limpets	10	
Lucines	15	
Limpets	5	
Margin Shells	25	
Mitres	25	
Moon Snails	15	
Murex Shells	10	
Mussels	5	
Nerite Snails	25	
Nut Shells	5	
Nutmegs	25	
Olives	25	

	Score	Date seen
Ormers	20	
Ostrich Foot Shells	25	
Pearl Oysters	25	
Pelican Foot Shells	20	
Periwinkles	5	
Piddocks	5	
Oysters	5	
Razor Shells	5	
Rock Shells	5	
Saddle Oysters	5	
Scallops	10	
Slipper Limpets	5	
Strombs	25	
Sundials	25	
Tellins	5	
Thorny Oysters	25	
Top Shells	10	
Trough Shells	10	
Tulip Shells	25	
Tun Shells	25	
Turban Shells	25	
Turrets	15	
Turrids	15	
Tusk Shells	15	
Vase Shells	25	

	Score	Date seen
Venus Clams	10	
Violet Shells	20	
Volutes	25	
Wedge Shells	5	
Wentletraps	15	
Whelks	10	
Worm Shells	25	

Index

Angel Wings, 46
Ark Shells, 37; Hairy, 37; Ponderous, 37
Angel's Wings, 46

Baby Ear, 15
Babylon, Channeled, 22
Banded Creeper, 13
Bitter Sweets, 37
Bivalves, 37-46; 51
Bleeding Tooth, 12
Bonnet, Japanese, 23; Scotch, 23
Bubble Shells, 36; Pacific, 36; White Banded, 36
Bull Mouth, 23
Bullia, Moroccan, 22
Button Shells, 34; Radiant, 34

Callidan, 18
Canoe Shell, 35
Carditao, 38; European, 38; Radiant, 38
Carrier Shells, 8; Mediterranean, 8; Pallid, 8
Cart Rut Shell, 20
Cephalopods, 49
Cerith, Common, 13
Chama, Leaf, 43
Chitons, 47; Lined, 47; Spiny, 47
Clams, Australian Surf, 45; Giant, 39; Violet Surf, 45
Cockles, 39; Dog, 37, Egg, 39; Spiny Paper, 39
Cock's Comb, 41
Conches, 24; 25; Crown, 27; Fighting, 24; Lister's, 24
Cone Shells, 28; Court, 28; Fig, 28; Prince, 28
Coquina, Giant False, 44; Panama, 44
Coral Snails, 21; Meyendorff's, 21; Violet, 21
Cowries, 34; Atlantic, 34; Egg, 35, Elongated Egg, 35; European, 34; False, 35; Humpback, 34; Little Deer, 34; Pustulate, 35; Sieve, 34
Crown Conches, 27
Crucibles, 7
Cup and Saucer, 7
Cuttlefish, 48

Distaff Spindle, 16
Dog Cockles, 37
Dog Whelks, 22; Unicolour, 22; Wolff's 22
Dove Shells, 36; Rustic, 36
Drupe, Red Mouth, 20
Duck Foot Shells, 26
Dye Shells, 20

Ear Shells, 9; Ridged, 9
Eastern Lion's Paw, 42

False Cowries, 35
False Tritons, 21; Giant, 21
Fan Mussels, 46
Fig Shells, 15; Spotted, 15
File Shells, 42; Iredale's Giant, 42
Foot Shells, Duck, 26; Ostrich, 26; Pelican, 26; West African Bird, 26
Frog Shells, 17; Blood Stained, 17

Gastropods, 6-36; 51; 53
Giant Clams, 39; Fluted, 39; Long, 39

Hairy Tritons, 17
Hallia, 33
Hammer Oysters, 40
Harp Shells, 28; Articulated, 28; Rose, 28;
Helmet Shells, 23; King, 23
Hoof Shells, 7
Horn Mouth, Leafy, 19
Horn Shells, 13
Horse's Hoof, 7
Hungarian Cap, 7

Jewel Boxes, 43

Keyhole Limpets, 6; Great Panama, 6; Italian, 6
Knorr's Worm, 14

Latirus, Knobbly, 16
Limpets, 6; Eye, 6; Italian, 6; Keyhole, 6; Mediterranean, 6; Slipper, 7; Tortoiseshell, 6
Little Fox, 29
Long Ancilla, 31
Lucines, 45; Buttercup, 45; Orb, 45

Mantle, 50
Margin Shells, 30; Desjardin's, 30; Loup, 30; Orange, 30; Philippine, 30; Pink, 30; Striper, 30
Mitres, 29; Cone, 29; Dactylus, 29; Diadem, 29; Thread, 29
Moon Snails, 15; Colourful Atlantic, 15; Lightning, 15
Murex Shells, 18; 19; Dye, 18; Pinnatus, 19; Ramose, 18; Stainforth's, 18; Zambo's, 19
Mussels, 38; Blue, 38; Date, 38; Fan, 46; Horse, 38; Yellow, 38

Nautilus, Brown Paper, 48; Chambered, 48; Paper, 48
Necklace Shells, 15

Needle Tooth, 16
Needle Whelks, 13
Neptune, New England, 22
Nerite Snails, 12; Chameleon, 12
Nut Shells, 37;
Nutmegs, 17; Common, 17

Olives, 31; Fat, 31; Lady, 31; Red Mouth, 31; Tent, 31
Operculum, 49; 51
Ormers, 9; Black, 9
Ostrich Foot Shells, 26
Oysters, 41; Flat, 40; Hammer, 40; Native, 41; Pearl, 40; Saddle, 41; Thorny, 43; White Hammer, 40

Pagoda, Mawa's, 21
Pearl Oysters, 40
Pelican Foot Shells, 26
Pelican's Tongue, 35
Pen Shells, 46
Periostracum, 50
Periwinkles, 12; Flat, 12; Southern, 12
Peruvian Hat, 7
Piddocks, 46
Purple Snail, Dwarf, 8

Radula, 51
Ramshorn, 48
Razor Shells, 46
Rock Shells, 20; Three Winged, 19; Wide Mouthed, 20
Roman Shield, 6

Saddle Oysters, 41
Sanguin, Stanger's, 45
Scallops, 42; Australian, 42; Calico, 42; Pilgrim's, 42
Screw Shells, 12; European, 12
Shark Eye, 15
Simnia, False, 35
Slipper Limpets, 7
Snipe Head, 26
Star Shells, 9; Modest, 9
Strombs, 24; 25; Granular, 24; Sail, 25; Scorpion, 24; Spider, 24
Sundials, 8; Giant, 8
Sunrise Shell, 44
Sunset Shells, 45
Surf Clam, Australian, 45; Violet, 45

Tellins, 44; Flat, 44
Thaid, Garland, 20
Thorny Oysters, 43; Red, 43
Tibia, Dwarf, 25; Martin's, 25; Powis', 25; Spindle, 25
Tooth Shell, Elephant, 47; Rosy, 47
Top Shells, 10; 11; Coral, 11; Dolphin, 11; Kelp, 10; Lined, 11; Pheasant, 11; Pyramid, 10; Radiant, 10; Snake Skin, 10; Strawberry, 10; Yellow Sponge, 10
Triton, Angular, 17; Atlantic, 17; Distorsio, 17; False, 21; Hairy, 17
Trough Shells, 45
Tulip Shells, 16; Fischer's, 16; Hunter's, 16
Tun Shells, 14; Banded, 14; Partridge, 14
Turban Shells, 9; Tapestry, 9
Turkey Wing, 37
Turrets, 12
Turrids, 14; Rose, 14
Tusk Shells, 48
Typhis, Cuming's, 19

Vase Shells, 26
Veliger, 51; 52
Venus Clams, 43; Keller's, 43; Lamellate, 43; Tent, 43
Venus Comb, 18
Violet Shells, 8
Volutes, 32-33; Algarve, 32; Beautiful, 33; Cuming's, 32; Ethiopian, 32; Damon's, 33; Hebrew, 32; Imperial, 32; Junonia, 3; Neptune, 33; Snowflake, 33

Wedge Shells, 44
Wentletraps, 13; Crenulated, 13; Precious, 13
Whelks, 23; Dog, 22; Fig, 27; Lightning, 27
Winkles, 12
Worm Shells, 14

HAMILTON COLLEGE